Colonial Inns and Taverns of

Bucks

COUNTY

In March 1683, William Penn's council ordered "The seal of the County of Bucks be a tree and a vine."
Courtesy of Bucks County Commissioners Office.

Colonial Inns and Taverns of Bucks County

How Pubs, Taprooms and Hostelries Made Revolutionary History

Marie Murphy Duess

The History Press

Published by The History Press
Charleston, SC 29403
www.historypress.net

Cover image courtesy of Center Bridge Inn, New Hope, Pennsylvania.

First published 2007
Second printing 2014

Manufactured in the United States

ISBN 978.1.59629.344.1

Library of Congress Cataloging-in-Publication Data
Duess, Marie Murphy.
Colonial inns and taverns of Bucks County, Pennsylvania : how pubs, taprooms and hostelries made Revolutionary history / Marie Murphy Duess.
vwp. cm.
Includes bibliographical references and index.
ISBN 978-1-59629-344-1 (alk. paper)
1. Taverns (Inns)--Pennsylvania--Bucks County--History. I. Title.
TX950.57.P4D94 2007
910.4609748'21--dc22
2007037724

To Ed, the love of my life…how wonderful it has been making history with you.

To my beautiful Mai-Ann and charming Buddy—my history and my future.

To Tommy and Christian, the two guys who keep me smiling.

And in memory of the 166 Continental Army soldiers buried in unmarked graves on a tiny tract of land in Langhorne…they are not forgotten.

Contents

Foreword

Bucks County is my home. For many who reside here, it is a source of pride to build our lives in such a fascinating place. Although much has been transformed and modernized in the last 230 years, what makes Bucks County special is its unique ability to hold its historic charm. Nowhere is that more visible than in the many taverns that still dot our landscape.

These taverns and inns continue to serve as central meeting places, as they did in the early days of our nation when patriots met to discuss the prospect of creating a new nation that aspired to guarantee freedom for all. While well-known cities and places were the sites of significant events during the Revolutionary War, Bucks County, its people and taverns quietly played a pivotal role in winning the freedom we cherish today.

Our history stretches back to well before the Revolutionary War. Pennsylvania's founder, William Penn, made his home in Bucks County. Our history in the Civil War era is also rich, serving as home to a number of stops along the Underground Railroad, leading many slaves to freedom.

This book will take you back in time and help you to "live" the experiences, which took place when Quakers arrived in the New World and patriots were willing to give their lives for a new nation. Later, area abolitionists risked everything to set a national wrong to right, all in the context of the inns and taverns that served as the social center of Bucks County communities.

Like William Penn, I have had the privilege and honor of leading the Commonwealth of Pennsylvania in my role as governor. As such, I have enjoyed being welcomed in the many cities, rural townships and historic boroughs of this wonderful state.

Those travels hold memories that I will always cherish. While these experiences will never be forgotten, the return trip home, after my time as governor had come to an end, was most special. I still remember the quiet drive that my wife, Kathy, and I enjoyed after departing the state capital to return home. Bucks County was as beautiful and vibrant as ever. As we passed through each village and town, its streets and taverns were bustling as they have been for centuries. We were home.

Foreword

Colonial Inns and Taverns of Bucks County, Pennsylvania: How Pubs, Taprooms and Hostelries Made Revolutionary History surely captures the essence of my home, Bucks County, and those less recognized establishments whose availability and ambience helped nourish a revolution and define a free nation. Through this book, I hope you enjoy your visit to our historic towns and taverns.

Mark S. Schweiker
Forty-fourth Governor of Pennsylvania
President & CEO, Greater Philadelphia Chamber of Commerce

Acknowledgements

Special thanks are extended to:
Mark Schweiker for taking time out of his busy summer to write the foreword for this book…he is a true son of Bucks County, a conscientious advocate for Philadelphia and was one of Pennsylvania's greatest governors.

Charles Lauble of the Historic Langhorne Association. His conscientious support and astounding knowledge were of utmost help in my research and acquisition of old photographs. His passion for the history of Langhorne is an inspiration.

The Newtown Historical Association—a treasure chest of research information. Their volunteers were most especially gracious and helpful during my many days and nights of researching this book. Special thanks go to Harriet Beckert, Richard Mansley, Heinz Heinemann, David Callahan and Brian Rounsavill.

Kim and Joe DaCosta of the Bridgetown Mill House and their gracious friends Rita and Lawrence Adair, Nancy Clark, Amy Clark and their maître d'hôtel, Loreto Mistretta, for their enthusiasm and smiles.

Geno and Amy Peruzzi and Jonathan and Elizabeth Hunt for the passion they all feel for their historic homes and for sharing that passion with me.

Bill Haas and Megan Hawk of Pen Ryn for sharing the incredible story of a graceful and valued old river mansion.

I am also indebted to:
Doug Miller, Tabitha Dardes, Margaret Scott, Susan Taylor, Amy E. Stock, Stacey Hajdak, Kathleen Kornell, Matt Buber, Ann Bartholomew, Kathleen Kornell, Bob Fried, Jerry Horan, Michael Reichert and the Faure family.

Rosanne Bell, BFF, Bucks County representative of the Pennsylvania Historical Society, for her friendship, her loveliness and her phone calls to whomever whenever I needed them.

Saunders Robinson, my editor, for her help, guidance and patience.

And to Greg Chalson…for the wonderful suggestion.

Finally, to the historians who spent so much of their lives recording Bucks County's history: W.W.H. Davis, A.M., J.H. Battle, Edward Barnsley, Willus Rivinus and Terry McNealy, and to all who wrote papers for the Bucks County Historical Society.

Part I

Early Days of Bucks County and its Public Houses

The country mansion of William Penn was established along the Delaware River in 1683. Pennsbury Manor consisted of a home, farm and outbuildings, and was the seat of government when Penn was in residence. *Courtesy of Pennsbury Manor, Fallsington, Pennsylvania, administered by the Pennsylvania Historical and Museum Commission.*

Introduction

The Legacy of William Penn

Let the people think they govern, and they will be governed!
—William Penn

No book about Bucks County can be written without telling the story of William Penn, the founder of the Commonwealth of Pennsylvania, a man who is considered to be one of this nation's greatest politicians. Nor can tales of Bucks County hospitality be told without discussing the first governor's mansion of Pennsylvania—Pennsbury—which William Penn built in Bucks County and where he hosted American Indian sachem, political dignitaries, European diplomats and Quaker meetings.

William Penn was a man who believed in the kind of liberty that was to eventually become a passionate cry for men and women of the American colonies. His "Holy Experiment" would set the groundwork for the American colonists' fight for independence.

Penn, an aristocrat with strong family ties to the Crown of England in the 1600s, took a different road than was expected of young men who belonged to the upper classes. He was highly intelligent and well educated, and he had a strong aversion to intolerance, especially when it came to religion. Even as a student in Oxford he rebelled against the religious interference of the Anglican Church in his studies and objected to being forced to attend Anglican services. He was deeply disillusioned by the many religious conflicts that plagued England.

Penn studied under the humanist Moïse Amyraut in France for a time, and returned to England as disheartened as he had been when he left. Perhaps his restlessness was a result of being exposed to the Society of Friends' philosophy when he was just a schoolboy living on his father's estates in Ireland, because he sought out more information about Quakerism as a young man and found that it answered questions for him that no other religion could. The Quakers' message of tolerance, the emphasis on a direct relationship with God and the belief that a person's conscience is the ultimate authority on morality (rather than the clergy, who interpreted the Scriptures) appealed to him, and he converted as a young man of twenty-three.

It was an unpopular decision—in fact, it was illegal to attend Quaker meetings at that time—and his conversion resulted in his being renounced and disowned by

William Penn (1644–1718), founder and proprietor of the colony King George II called Pennsylvania, was a Quaker and renowned diplomat and statesman. *Courtesy of Pennsbury Manor, Fallsington, Pennsylvania, administered by the Pennsylvania Historical and Museum Commission.*

his own father, Admiral William Penn. Yet, the younger Penn remained true to his convictions even when they brought him great persecution.

Penn's campaign for justice and fair trials in England were often successful, and based on facts and arguments presented to court by William Penn, the lord chief justice of England ruled that juries were not to be coerced or punished for their verdicts. It was an important victory for William Penn, and after the ruling his popularity grew. He drew huge crowds when he spoke publicly, and he was invited to visit Quaker communities across Europe. He was arrested several times for speaking out against the Anglican Church, and he even spent several months in the Tower of London.

Between arrests and prison terms, Penn fell in love and married Gulielma Springett, an only child of a wealthy Quaker couple, and they were to have seven children, four of whom died in infancy. Because of his experiences and the persecution he witnessed in England, William Penn longed for a place where people would have the right to worship as they wanted and live in peace and acceptance.

Then, when his father died in 1670 and Penn inherited the family landholdings in Ireland, it came to his attention that the Crown owed a monetary debt to his father. He realized that this was his chance to act on his belief that people should have the right to a place where they could worship as they wanted and follow their own consciences. He asked King Charles II for a charter to establish a colony in America in repayment for the debt owed to him on behalf of his father. The king signed that charter for the land he called the "Woods of Penn"—or "Pennsylvania"—and appointed William the proprietor of the land, accountable to the king directly.

After receiving the charter, even before he left for America, William Penn developed the *First Frame of Government*, which provided, first and foremost, religious toleration, as well as secured private property, unlimited free enterprise, a free press and trial by jury—principles expressed nearly one hundred years later in the Declaration of Independence and the United States Constitution. (Thomas Jefferson once declared William Penn to be the "greatest lawgiver of all time.")[1]

In 1682 he left Ireland aboard the *Welcome*, eager to implement what he called the "Holy Experiment." Now he would have an opportunity to establish a government based on religious tolerance, free of bickering between denominations, and establish a form of rule that would have an enormous influence on America's founding fathers.

Penn's religious tolerance would extend beyond the Society of Friends to the Germans, Swedes, Dutch and Native Americans who already lived within the boundaries of the new colony, and he was diligent in making certain that the residents of Pennsylvania were aware of the positive changes he would bring about as proprietor. In a letter to colonists who were already living in Pennsylvania, William Penn wrote:

> *For you are now fixed at the mercy of no governor that comes to make his fortune great; you shall be governed by laws of your own making and live a free, and if you will, a sober and industrious life. I shall not usurp the right of any, or oppress his person. God has furnished me with a better resolution and has given me his grace to keep it.*[2]

In November 1682, under a wide spreading elm tree, William Penn concluded a just treaty with American Indian chiefs of the Lenni-Lenape tribes, an agreement which was upheld by all throughout Penn's lifetime. *Courtesy of Historical Documents Company.*

In the freedoms and rights the *First Frame of Government* afforded, there were just two offenses that would require the death penalty—murder and treason—and he established peaceful change through amendments. In Penn's colony women were encouraged to seek education and speak out as equals with men.

Penn's savvy political leadership was marked by the fact that instead of stealing land from the Delaware Native American tribes—the Shawnees, Susquehannocks and Lenape—he initiated the "Great Treaty" with them and purchased land from the American Indians through peaceful negotiations. He learned their dialects, walked among them without guards and offered them friendship and fair trade. He was rewarded with their respect, and this mutual admiration and trust between Penn and the Native Americans lasted for more than seventy years.

The desire for religious freedom in England and other parts of Europe was strong and by the end of 1683, fifty shiploads of immigrants had reached the colony of Pennsylvania. Additionally, Penn campaigned to persuade all persons interested in economic opportunity and freedom from religious persecution to immigrate to the colony by offering five-thousand-acre tracts of land at one hundred pounds per tract. Most of the early settlers were English and Welsh Quakers but also included Dutch, German and Scotch-Irish, followed by Moravians, Mennonites and Huguenots. Pennsylvania was the only place under British rule where Catholics were legally allowed to worship in public. By the time the American Revolution began, the population of Pennsylvania had grown to nearly three hundred thousand and was one of the largest colonies in America with the most diverse population.

PENNSBURY MANOR

Even before he arrived from Ireland, Penn had his cousin, William Markham, choose a tract of land on which to build Penn's home along the banks of the graceful Delaware River in what was to become the first of three original counties, called Buckinghamshire, later shortened to Bucks County. Penn issued orders of how he wanted the construction of the site to proceed, giving specific directives about the construction of the building as well as detailed instructions to the gardener, Ralph Smyth. His home was to reflect his personal tastes and his great love of nature.

He intended to bring his family from Britain and spend his remaining life at Pennsbury, and it was important to him that the rooms be spacious and inviting with views of the countryside. As proprietor of Pennsylvania he would host dignitaries, and as a Quaker he would host Quaker meetings when he couldn't get away to the local meetinghouse.

Penn appointed James Harrison to be the overseer of Pennsbury. He hired several skilled servants, but contrary to his strong belief in the individual right of freedom, he also had indentured and enslaved servants working at Pennsbury, both during the construction of the property and after.

Although it was necessary for Penn to maintain a place in the city of Philadelphia while he was involved in the daily planning of that city's development, he relished

Even before arriving in the colony, William Penn gave explicit instructions about the gardens: "Set out the garden by the house, plant sweet herbs, asparagus, carrots…and all flowers and kitchen herbs there." *Courtesy of Pennsbury Manor, administered by the Pennsylvania Historical and Museum Commission.*

any time spent at his country manor. He traveled by barge on the Delaware from Philadelphia to the banks of his graceful Pennsbury, spending the summer months surrounded by the natural environment he loved. He once wrote, "The country life is to be preferred, for there we see the works of God." He longed to bring his wife and children from England to the home he was making for them at Pennsbury. "A country life and estate," he wrote to Gulielma, "I like best for my children."[3]

Penn was a man with excellent political instinct. He was able to remain influential in England even as he established himself in the colonies. He was a diplomat that continued a close friendship with the king of England, even while recruiting English subjects to his colony by offering them the liberty that the Crown and the Church of England was refusing them. He traveled through neighboring colonies, visited Quaker communities and called on other political leaders, earning their respect and admiration.

Unfortunately, this was not the case with Lord Baltimore in Maryland. His visit there was troublesome because of a dispute over the boundary between Pennsylvania and Maryland. They both returned to England to register appeals with the king, and shortly after Penn's arrival back in England, his friend James II succeeded to the throne. James, a convert to Catholicism, had promised religious freedom for nonconformists, and Penn became an advisor to the monarch hoping that England would become a more tolerant nation under James's rule. Those hopes were dashed when James fell and William and Mary ascended, leaving William Penn in danger of being arrested again.

Forced to live in seclusion, and even imprisoned as a traitor for a time, Penn's fortunes began to decline and he was detained from returning to his colony in the New World with

The Delaware River was the easiest means of travel to Pennsbury from Philadelphia for people, livestock, goods and building supplies. Brick steps covered in stone were built at the end of the upper court for access to the property. *Courtesy of Pennsbury Manor, administered by the Pennsylvania Historical and Museum Commission.*

his family. Sadly, his wife Gulielma died before she could see the home her husband had built for her and their three living children, Springett, Letitia and William Jr.

Penn found solace in the presence of his friend, Hannah Callowhill, who was twenty-seven years younger than he. They were married in 1696, and William Penn returned to Pennsylvania with his bride and grown daughter Letitia in 1699. The first of their children, John, was born in Pennsylvania—the only American-born child of William Penn.

Hannah became mistress of the red brick mansion with ease, and she and her stepdaughter took great care in managing Pennsbury while in residence there. One guest wrote of her, "The governor's wife and daughter are well...his wife is extremely well-beloved here, and exemplary in her station...and she has great place in the hearts of good people."[4]

Once again, Pennsbury was to become the scene of William Penn's hospitality to Europeans and American Indians alike, as well as governors of other colonies. He reestablished friendly relationships with the Native Americans, and they gathered at Pennsbury to review the covenants that had been made between the white man and the American Indian nations of Pennsylvania. The meeting was both amicable and successful. Nineteen Native American treaties had been concluded in all. In *The History of Bucks County Pennsylvania*, W.W.H. Davis reports:

> *There is a tradition, that when the Indians came to visit him at Pennsbury, William Penn joined them in their sports and games, and ate hominy, venison and roasted acorns with them. He is said to have matched them in strength and agility.*[5]

It took approximately five hours by barge (similar to this replica) for Pennsbury residents and guests to reach the manor from Philadelphia, utilizing a mast and sail as well as several oarsmen. *Courtesy of Pennsbury Manor, administered by the Pennsylvania Historical and Museum Commission.*

While the family was in residence at Pennsbury the manor thrived, as did his work. Penn signed into law the Charter of Privileges, which enabled the Pennsylvania General Assembly to initiate legislation and thereby permitted the people to be governed by laws of their own making. The charter, which remained the constitution of the colony until the American Revolution, guaranteed religious freedom and separation of church and state.

But not all was well in England, and there were threats in Parliament to terminate Penn's proprietorship. He was forced to return to England just two years after arriving in his beloved colony for the second time. He urged Hannah and Letitia to remain in Pennsylvania since he expected to return immediately, but Hannah refused to stay without him.

He sent his son, William Jr., to Pennsylvania in order to acquaint him with the responsibilities of governing the land that the young man would inherit one day, but although William Jr. did stay at Pennsbury for a while, the country life was too quiet for him as he preferred a more social life. He returned to Philadelphia, and shortly after that, sailed back to England less than a year after arriving.

William and Hannah were to have more children after returning to England. Hannah gave birth to Thomas, Margaret, Richard, Dennis and Hannah.

Because of his increasing financial difficulties, Penn was unable to send funding for the land or the buildings at Pennsbury. He was forced to sell off portions of the property and had to let many of the servants at Pennsbury go, keeping just a small group of caregivers to oversee the upkeep of the manor house. He worried constantly about the home he longed to return to, but William Penn was never to see Pennsbury again, as he was never to return to America. His poverty and ill health prevented it. He died in 1718, and his beloved Pennsbury fell to ruin because of neglect. Half of the title to Pennsylvania passed to his son John, the only child born in America, and the other half was divided among John's brothers. John never married, and when he died his share in the title to Pennsylvania went to his brother Thomas.

Thomas, and afterward his nephews, John and Richard, governed Pennsylvania during the eighteenth century as absentee proprietors. Pennsylvania remained a proprietary colony in the Penn family until the Revolution. Penn's grandson, Richard Penn, had purchased three hundred acres at Pennsbury intending to build a home there, but the American Revolution prevented that from happening. No Penn ever lived at Pennsbury again.

In 1803, Robert Crozier purchased three hundred acres and built a large frame farmhouse on part of the original foundation of the manor house, farmed the land and it remained in the Crozier's ownership until the 1880s. Eventually, ownership transferred to the Penn Warner Company, which operated a gravel quarry close to the site.

On the 250th anniversary of William Penn's arrival in America, October 23, 1932, the Penn Warner Company donated a ten-acre parcel that included the site of the manor house to the Commonwealth of Pennsylvania, and it was then turned over to the Pennsylvania Historical Commission.

The Crozier farmhouse was moved to another part of the site and archeological excavations began in search of the original foundations and any fragments and pieces of the original Pennsbury Manor. Archeologist Dr. Donald A. Cadzoe oversaw the excavations that unearthed bricks, nails, hinges, panes of glass from the original windows and delft tiles that had framed the fireplaces. Using letters and notes from William Penn to James Logan and James Harrison, Pennsbury's overseer, and others who had received instructions about the construction of the original buildings at Pennsbury, William Penn's lovely red brick manor house was completely reconstructed under the guidance of R. Brognard Okie, a renowned Pennsylvanian restoration architect. Whenever possible, the original artifacts were used in the reconstruction, including the window glass and delft tiles. Shortly after the reconstruction of both the manor house and the bake and brew house was completed, the commonwealth purchased an additional thirty acres and reconstructed other outbuildings and the landscaping that had once graced the grounds of Pennsbury.

Today, Pennsbury Manor is administered by the Pennsylvania Historical and Museum Commission in collaboration with the Pennsbury Society. The grounds contain original and reconstructed structures, formal and kitchen gardens and the types

Pennsbury fell into ruin after the death of William Penn and the Penn family's subsequent financial decline. In the 1930s the manor was completely reconstructed using letters Penn had written with detailed instructions for its layout. *Courtesy of Pennsbury Manor, administered by the Pennsylvania Historical and Museum Commission.*

of animals that would have been a part of the original farm. Living history programs are scheduled throughout the year with demonstrations that include blacksmithing, open-hearth cooking and sheepshearing.

"Whatever sober and free man can reasonably desire for the security and improvement of their own happiness, I shall heartily comply with," William Penn, the first governor of the Commonwealth of Pennsylvania stated.[6] Although he was a man of vision, spirituality, intelligence and idealism, he suffered greatly because of his trust in the goodness of other people's consciences. He was a modest man, a great diplomat, and the Constitution of the United States and the freedoms and rights we enjoy today are testament to the value of this gentle man's "Holy Experiment." The pursuit of liberty—the purity at liberty's core—is the legacy William Penn has left to America, and his desire that "the will of one man may not hinder the good of a whole country" lives in all Americans.

On November 28, 1984, President Ronald Reagan, upon an act of Congress, granted William Penn and his wife Hannah honorary citizenship in the United States of America.

The fireplace in the large entrance hall at Pennsbury was reconstructed using tiles found during the archeological dig on the site. *Courtesy of Pennsbury Manor, administered by the Pennsylvania Historical and Museum Commission.*

The Infamous Walking Purchase Began in Bucks County

When William Penn took over proprietorship of Pennsylvania, his "Holy Experiment" not only reached out to the settlers who lived in Pennsylvania, but extended to the Native Americans who had been the stewards of the land long before the Europeans arrived. The treaty of 1682 with the Delaware chiefs at Shackamaxon, north of Philadelphia, has been celebrated in song, poetry and art. It is considered a model of mutual respect and fair play. Through fair negotiations, Penn purchased land from the American Indians instead of claiming the land as his own and fighting territorial wars with them. Unlike the other American colonies, which were plagued with bloody wars with Native Americans, Pennsylvania enjoyed a peaceful coexistence with the local tribes that lasted more than sixty years.

William Penn's honest and fair dealings with the Lenape American Indians came to an end when Penn's sons, John and Thomas, assumed proprietorship of Pennsylvania.

Relations with the Lenape were already strained in William Penn's absence when Governor William Keith had invited squatters from the Hudson River Valley to settle on American Indian owned lands along the upper Delaware River. Additionally, Lenape lands were being usurped by refugee Native American tribes by the Six Nation Iroquois.

William Penn met with dignitaries, aristocrats and American Indian chiefs in his office at Pennsbury when in residence during summer months. He and his wife Hannah even hosted Quaker meetings in their home. *Courtesy of Pennsbury Manor, administered by the Pennsylvania Historical and Museum Commission.*

The English regarded the Iroquois nation as a strong ally in blocking French expansion, and the Pennsylvania government encouraged their encroachment upon the Lenape.

John and Thomas Penn were in need of funds to satisfy their creditors. They hoped to raise money by selling land that was located in the forks of the Delaware just north of Bucks County, which was owned by the Lenape, to a growing number of German and Scotch-Irish settlers. They presented an old, incomplete and unsigned draft of a deed dating back to the 1680s to the Lenape, claiming that the deed had been signed by Lenape chiefs. The document stated that the land to be deeded to the Penns was as much as could be covered in a day-and-a-half walk.

Unsure about the validity of the deed, the Lenape chiefs reluctantly agreed to what is now called "The Walking Purchase," thinking that the most a man could walk through the wilderness in a day and a half was about forty miles. They were unaware that Penn's longtime secretary, James Logan, had planned the "walk" by hiring the three fastest runners in the colony, Edward Marshall, Solomon Jennings and James Yeates. Additionally, the trail had been prepared beforehand, the grass leveled and the fastest route plotted.

On September 19, 1737, the three athletes gathered before dawn at a chestnut tree near the Wrightstown Quaker Meeting House, and as the sun rose, they began to run west from

A monument on the grounds of Wrightstown Meetinghouse reads: To the memory of the Lenni-Lenape Indians. Ancient owners of this region. These stones are placed at this spot. The starting point of the Indian Walk, September 19, 1737. *Author Collection.*

Wrightstown, stopping only to sleep for the night. The pace was intense and they moved steadily, without stopping. The Native Americans who followed them complained that the walk didn't follow the Delaware River, which they believed had been agreed upon, and that the "walkers" were cheating since they were not walking at a normal pace. Their complaints fell on deaf ears. Jennings collapsed mid-morning of the first day, and the other two continued their exhausting pace until 6:15 that evening, after covering forty-five miles. The second day dawned cold and rainy. Yates dropped out after a fall in the creek left him temporarily blinded. Marshall continued on and finished at two o'clock in the afternoon, after covering a total of sixty-seven miles.

The surveyors who had accompanied the party set about surveying the upper line of the purchase, and the Native Americans charged that the line was not run at right angles in the direction of the walk, but in a northeast direction. The result was that the land obtained by the walk amounted to approximately 1,200,000 acres, an area roughly equivalent to the size of the state of Rhode Island. The area of the purchase covers all or part of what are now Pike, Monroe, Carbon, Schuylkill, Northampton, Lehigh and Bucks counties.

Although they felt that they had been cheated by the Penns, the Lenape were honor bound to agree to the purchase. However, the Walking Purchase of 1737 was one of the principal reasons for the alienation of the Delaware American Indians after so many years of peaceful agreement. As a result of the Walking Purchase, the American Indian tribes of Pennsylvania joined the French against the English colonies in the French and Indian War that was fought in the 1750s.

Solomon Jennings returned to his home near Bethlehem, and it took him a full year to recover from the exhausting effects of the walk. Edward Yates was blinded for three days after he fell during the walk. He never fully regained his health and died within a year.

As for Edward Marshall, the Penns had promised him a grant of five hundred acres for completing the walk. He never received this grant. After the Revolutionary War, he was awarded a total of one hundred and twenty-eight acres for his service to the colony. He was never forgiven by the Native American tribes because of his participation in the Walking Purchase.

Under the proprietorship of William Penn, no white blood had been shed by angry American Indians. The Walking Purchase changed that considerably, and Edward Marshall was to feel the brunt of that anger. While he was away from home one day, a raiding party of sixteen Native Americans attacked his home and killed his wife Elizabeth and their unborn child. Marshall moved back to Bucks County to live on an island in the Delaware, but he still could not escape the wrath of the Native Americans and they continued to harass him. He eventually remarried and had twenty-one children, but the eldest, Peter, was also killed in a Native American attack. Marshall died at the age of seventy-nine.

Chapter 1

Native Trails to Roads of Progress

May you have the hindsight to know where you've been, the foresight to know where you're going and the insight to know when you're going too far.
—An Irish toast

Early Settlements

The first inhabitants of the fertile river valley along the Delaware, which we now call Bucks County, were the Lenape—a wolf tribe that lived in relative peace and enjoyed the beauty of the land for many years before the Europeans arrived. It was upon their footpaths that the roads in Bucks County were built.

European exploration of the Delaware River Valley began in 1609 with Henry Hudson. In 1610, English captain Samuel Argall named the river after the governor of Virginia, Thomas West, Lord De La Warr. Then a fifty-four-year-old English captain, Thomas Yong, began an exploration of the Americas in search of the Northwest Passage at his own expense on behalf of England with permission of King Charles I. He landed first in Jamestown, Virginia, and remained there for two weeks while one of his two vessels was being repaired. Eager to complete his exploration, he set sail north to Delaware Bay and traveled up the Delaware River as far as the falls, which is near what is now called Morrisville.

Unable to continue beyond the falls, Captain Yong was forced to leave, but not before exploring much of the land along the river and establishing good relationships with the local American Indian tribes. He sent a report to the king telling him that he intended to build a vessel that would bring him above the falls so that he could continue to explore the "Charles River," which he temporarily renamed in honor of the king. His Native American friends who had traveled north on the river reported beautiful mountains and lakes, and Yong was certain that the "Charles" would lead him to the Mediterranean Sea. In his report to the king, he described the beauty of the land in great detail, wrote about the fruits that grow wild, with specific mention of plums and grapes, and the abundant number of game and fowl. His promise to move even farther upriver wasn't to be kept, however, and he left the Delaware Valley to continue his exploration on the Hudson River.

The scenic 410-mile-long Delaware River, constituting the entire boundary between Pennsylvania and New Jersey and a portion of New York, is one of the major waterways in the region, navigable by large oceangoing vessels. *Author Collection.*

European traders and trappers, who had arrived in the New World shortly after its discovery, were very familiar with the dense forests of the Delaware Valley, and no doubt gave vivid descriptions of the fertile lands and plentiful game located in the woodlands and meadows of the graceful river valley to the towns and trading centers they visited. In response, scattered settlements were established by Swedish, Dutch and German immigrants years before Charles II gave the land charter to William Penn.

The first documented land grant falling within Bucks County was to a New Yorker named Samuel Edsall. It was an island called Sankhickans, and Edsall received the grant from the governor of "New Netherland," who oversaw governorship of the region at that time. Years later, in 1679, several Quaker families crossed the Delaware from New Jersey and settled in an area that they called Crewcorne, which was located near the falls that deterred Captain Yong from farther travel upriver.

One of the earliest settlers in the region, James Boyden, who belonged to the group of Swedish families that had settled on the Delaware long before Penn was given the charter, was one of the first representatives of Bucks County in the assembly. An account in J.H. Battle's *History of Bucks County* once again affirms the peaceful coexistence of the Native Americans with the white settlers here. The Boyden family had adopted and reared a little girl. One of her chores was to tend the cattle and keep them from wandering in the swamps along the Delaware River. Battle writes, "One rainy time she was lost, and wandered in the wet three days and nights until too weak to go farther, when she lay down and cried. An Indian heard her, and carried her home. She always retained a peculiar friendship and esteem for the natives, having learned their language in her infancy." It would have been difficult to learn the language of the Native American tribe in the short period of time that she was carried home by this gentle and caring American Indian, so we can only assume that this friendship continued long after her life was saved by the compassionate native.

The Delaware River has always been a life source for the region, and the valley was rich with fruits and game. In his *History of Bucks County*, J.H. Battle quotes a letter by a settler named Claypoole who wrote to a friend in 1681:

> *I have seen orchards laden with fruit to admiration, their very limbs torn to pieces with their weight, and most delicious to the taste, and lovely to behold…It is my judgment by what I have observed, that fruit trees in this country destroy themselves by the very weight of their fruit: As for venison and fowls, we have great plenty: We have brought home to our houses by the Indians, seven or eight fat bucks of a day…and fish in their season are very plenteous…As to the beef and pork, here is plenty of it, and cheap.*[7]

Correspondence similar to this from other settlers was incentive enough for Europeans to long for their own acreage in the New World.

The opportunity to fulfill this dream of owning land in America became available when, after receiving the charter from Charles II and even before leaving for America himself, William Penn lodged a campaign to persuade all who were interested in freedom from religious persecution as well as economic opportunity to purchase tracts of land in Pennsylvania. The immigrants were offered five-thousand-acre tracts at one hundred pounds per tract and the additional incentive of five hundred acres of land in Philadelphia for every five thousand acres of land purchased outside the city, thereby encouraging greater areas of settlement. English, Welsh and Irish Quakers were the first to take advantage of this opportunity followed by the Dutch, German and Scotch-Irish.

The first immigrants to sail directly to Pennsylvania left England in 1681 in several ships. The first ship to arrive was the *John and Sarah*, and according to historian W.W. Davis in his *History of Bucks County*, passengers who arrived on that ship were called "first landers" by those who followed a short time after.

In most cases, the immigrants purchased the land before they left Europe, and once they arrived in America, they settled near the mouth of the Delaware, following ports along the river that were large enough to accommodate seagoing vessels. They moved up the river from New Castle, through Wilmington, Philadelphia, Chester and farther upstream at the Bucks County port of Bristol, and when they reached the falls in Morrisville, they turned inland and followed tributaries such as the Neshaminy Creek.

Although heavily forested with no roads to follow but the footpaths of the Lenni-Lenape, the early settlers who persevered were rewarded by the rich soil afforded to them by the well-irrigated meadows. Determined to make new homes for

The Moon-Williamson log house, ca.1750, stands on its original site in Fallsington. Colonists used clay and animal hair to close in the gaps between the logs. *Courtesy of Historic Fallsington, Inc.*

their families in America, they worked day and night to turn these meadows into lush pastures and productive farms.

The Quakers settled primarily in the southeastern part of Bucks County, nearer to Bristol and up through Newtown to Wrightstown. The English followed the Delaware River north, and the Scotch-Irish settled northeast across the central part of the county. The German settlements were located in the northwest corner.

The immigrants built their homes according to their own tradition. The Swedes built log homes, and depending upon their financial circumstances, they added planked ceilings and one or two glass windows. The English built frame houses using clapboards that they either sawed by hand or purchased from the mills in New Jersey. Unfortunately, the wood was usually green when the homes were built and in time shrunk on the frame of the house. Clay mixed with animal hair covered the openings left by the shrinking boards to protect the inhabitants from the harsh winter environment. As evidenced by the many remaining structures that dot the Bucks County landscape today, many homes of that era were built of fieldstone, which was probably collected when the family cleared the land for planting crops.

Most of the homes were of one or two rooms, usually with a loft above. Footholds were carved into the walls for climbing up into the lofts where children or servants slept. The main room usually had a fireplace for cooking, sometimes a tiny larder, and

This Taylorsville building is an excellent representation of the type of stone buildings that provided shelter for Quaker and other European colonists. *Courtesy of Washington Crossing Historic Park, administered by the Pennsylvania Historical and Museum Commission.*

it served as the kitchen, sitting room and often the master bedroom. Families were large, and it wasn't uncommon for as many as ten or more adults and children to occupy a tiny house.

In the seventeenth-century colonies, travel in this region was easier on the Delaware and its tributaries than it was by land. Ferries and ferry taverns sprouted up from Philadelphia to Bristol and points beyond, and they offered a brief respite for the early immigrants. Trade on the river grew, and in time products from the colonies were shipped in exchange for merchandise from abroad. Salt, sugar, molasses, rum, hardware and even a few luxuries were imported by American merchants from places like the West Indies and Barbados, and the farmers exchanged whatever produce and goods they could spare to trade for the products brought to America from abroad. Those products were moved by river primarily to Burlington, New Jersey—at that time a major port.

The Development of Roads

Pennsylvania's first roads were the footpaths made and traveled by the American Indians. As inland settlements grew, it became necessary for these imports to be transported overland from the river ports using pack trains—horses or mules laden

Early homes in colonial America consisted of one room, which was used as a kitchen, dining room, master bedroom and nursery. There was often a loft above, where the children and slaves slept. *Courtesy of Pennsbury Manor, administered by the Pennsylvania Historical and Museum Commission.*

with goods. After the Europeans arrived and as settlement advanced many of the old paths were widened, first for the white man's pack trains and then for his wagons.

Once again, William Penn's skillful proprietorship is evident in the fact that immediately following the receipt of the land grant from King Charles II in 1681, even while still in England, he formed an agreement with various purchasers of land in Pennsylvania that stipulated, "Great roads from City to City not to contain less than forty feet in breadth shall be first laid out and declared to be for highways."[8]

An act of the general assembly in 1683 required that each county court appoint overseers every fall to build highways and bridges. Roads were laid out from Philadelphia throughout Bucks County and north into Easton. Those roads joined the roads being built between Philadelphia and New York, opening travel wider and thereby promoting stronger trade between colonies and further settlement. Most roads, particularly local, were not so much built as simply cleared, with perhaps a little digging on the sides of hills or the erection of rough wooden bridges over smaller streams. The most durable roads were made of crushed stone and proved to be the best suited for the harsh weather of the eastern United States.

The first road was the King's Path (or King's Road as it is sometimes called), which was established around 1677 between Frankford and Morrisville and was a section of the route between Philadelphia and New York. Old York Road opened in 1711

Colonials transported products and goods to markets in Philadelphia and Burlington, New Jersey, first by pack trains and then by rough-hewn wagons pulled over early roads in Bucks County that were difficult if not impossible to navigate. *Author Collection.*

on the path of an American Indian trail from Jenkintown to Center Bridge through Hatboro and Buckingham. Easton Road was established in the 1720s and traveled from Horsham to Easton. Durham Road was built in two sections and took from 1693 to 1746 to complete; the first section was built between Bristol and Newtown, then on to the Durham Iron Furnace to the north. Bethlehem Road was opened in 1738 in the northwestern region of Bucks County.

Maintenance of the "King's Highways" was sporadic at best, and "turnpikes" were formed and tolls were collected for travel on these roads, which were to be used to maintain them. The road system in Pennsylvania became challenged when the canals were built during the first half of the nineteenth century. Mule teams pulled cargo-laden boats along the canal, and as America expanded, the canals provided a more convenient and economical way of transporting coal to urban areas such as Philadelphia and New York.

With the introduction of the steam engine and rail lines, roads became even less important. For long-distance and intercity transportation of both passengers and freight, people turned from the highways to the "iron horse." Then in the late 1800s electric trolley car lines became an even more popular mode of transportation.

With insufficient revenue to maintain them, the main thoroughfares and turnpikes fell into disrepair and became victims of progress, and many of the taverns and inns

The Durham Pike Tollhouse was the home of the gatekeeper's family. The gate was lowered until the toll was collected. Originally on Sycamore and Durham road, it was moved to its present location in 1955 by Goodnoe Dairies. *Author Collection.*

that had flourished once upon a time were closed or became markets or private homes. However, progress in the form of the automobile was to change that situation for good, and once again the need for well-maintained roads and stopping points along the way grew steadily from just after the turn of the century.

Old roads were repaired and expanded, and new roads were established. Small villages grew into towns, and new municipalities sprung up along the new roads. Although it had retained its rural landscape for most of the twentieth century, Bucks County reflects the steady growth and prosperity of recent years, and the roads that were once footpaths of the Lenape are being expanded once again to handle the overflow of traffic.

Protective of its history and charm, many of the towns and cities in Bucks County have maintained and renovated the taverns and inns that served the early settlers in the county, and they still sit gracefully beside the old highways and byways, inviting the weary traveler in for some rest, nourishment and if so inclined, a good mug of ale.

Chapter 2

The Signs of the Time

Better one byrde in the hande than ten in the wood.
—John Heywood, 1546

The Importance of Taverns in Colonial America

With the establishment of the roads, inland taverns also became essential. Larger towns were expected to have lodging for travelers and could even be fined if they didn't provide accommodations. Savvy settlers made their homes available to weary travelers for a fee, offering a good meal accompanied by ale or rum, which no doubt helped to make what was often just a straw-filled comforter thrown near a fireplace seem a more comfortable bed for the night.

Public houses were built along the major new highways that crisscrossed Bucks County. The taverns, which were also called "ordinaries" in the sixteenth and early seventeenth centuries, became the centers of social life, and just about every village had a tavern or two (or more) depending upon the size of the town, its location and its importance. Next to the church, the tavern was the most important building in town. In fact, many taverns were built in communities long before the foundation was ever laid for the church. When there was no church building, the tavern would be used for church services. They also were used as courtrooms for traveling justices, meeting places for militia, polling places for elections, lecture halls for politicians, ballrooms for weddings and dances and very often for public auctions.

Normally taverns and inns were located at the crossing of two roads, and when possible, close to water—a stream, tributary or the river. In the early years, most Bucks County taverns were used primarily by farmers and drovers taking their produce to markets in Philadelphia or Trenton. Respectable innkeepers were often influential in the town, and because they were constantly in touch with travelers, could relate news of other localities (or gossip if they were so inclined). In some cases, innkeepers held political positions in a town or became justices of the peace and wardens of the law—their inns were used as jailhouses.

The importance of the tavern in early America is also apparent in the fact that it wasn't uncommon for a locality to be called by the name of the local establishment.

Used as a pub name in the United Kingdom since the Middle Ages, "bird in hand" became just as popular for taverns in colonial America. This sign is a reproduction of one painted for a tavern in Newtown. *Author Collection.*

Above and below: The Langhorne Hotel before the two-story porch was added and after. These structures were added to catch the mail as stagecoach drivers threw it high and fast from the coach when they weren't stopping. *Courtesy of the Langhorne Historic Association.*

The Ox Inn, which was located on what was called the Lincoln Highway between Middletown and Falls Townships, was in operation before 1773. It was a popular tavern, and the village became known as Oxford. This region of Bucks County has retained that name. Where Doyle's Tavern was built, the area was subsequently called Doylestown.

As overland travel grew, so did the taverns, sometimes to three stories high, although most were two-story buildings. Usually constructed of fieldstone, there were two front doors—one for the barroom and the other opened into the receiving room where ladies and families entered. As stagecoaches became the vehicle for transporting mail and freight, two-story front porches were added to the buildings so that stagecoach drivers could toss mailbags to the second story of the porch without stopping.

The interiors of the smaller taverns usually consisted of one public room with a small bar in the corner to dispense beverages. That area was normally called the "bar and grill" since a locked wooden grid was put down around the bar whenever the bartender had to leave his station to prevent the liquor from being "borrowed" in his absence. This room also contained a number of tables where groups of people could eat family style. The kitchen, which was at the rear of the tavern or in the basement, was very often the focal point of the building, especially during cold months when exhausted travelers could find comfort in the warmth of the large fireplace where the food was prepared. There were small rooms on the upper floors for overnight guests, and it wasn't unusual for guests to have to share not only a room with strangers, but the bed as well. Less prosperous patrons slept on the kitchen floor near the hearth, which in the long run may have been the warmest room in the house since the backlog—a large log that burned all night—was set in the rear of the fireplace so that it would not have to be relighted in the morning.

Outbuildings usually included stables, barns for farm animals, springhouses, smokehouses, icehouses and "necessaries" (outhouses), which served both the travelers and innkeeper's family. Smart innkeepers made sure that their establishment had the capabilities to shoe horses and repair wagon wheels.

Running a tavern and inn was a family affair. Most innkeepers were also farmers, and the food that was served from the kitchen came from their farms and gardens. Their children usually helped with the farm chores, while the innkeepers minded the taproom. Innkeepers' wives were involved in all aspects of the tavern except the bar. They oversaw the cooking, cleaning of the rooms and service to the patrons. The quality of the inn, its cleanliness and character, reflected the woman who oversaw the activities behind the scenes. The children were expected to wait tables, clean stables and help with patrons' horses when their parents were busy in the tavern. It wasn't unusual for an innkeeper's wife to continue to operate the inn as a licensed holder after her husband's death, especially if the facility was well established and highly regarded.

According to *Early Taverns of Bucks County* by Willis Rivinus, inns sometimes received a letter of introduction from the guest before the person arrived. A note of this kind by Benjamin Franklin to an innkeeper reads:

Typical "bar and grill" where patrons were served beverages. Food was prepared in a kitchen located at the back of the building or in the "cellar." *Courtesy Washington Crossing Historic Park, administered by the Pennsylvania Historical and Museum Commission.*

> *To the ever curious landlord and his assembled staff—*
> *Worthy people, I am Benjamin Franklin of Philadelphia, by trade a printer, and bachelor. I have some relatives in Boston to whom I am going to make a visit; my stay will be short, and I shall then return and follow my business as a prudent man ought to. This is all I know of myself and all I can possibly inform you of. I beg therefore you will have pity on me and my horse and give us both refreshments.*[9]

Stagecoach Stops

Not all taverns were equal. In fact, there were class distinctions among them. In 1766, the first stagecoaches from the Swift-Sure Stage Line started serving travelers in the region, and regular stage service between Easton and Philadelphia was established by the early 1790s, requiring the establishment of numerous stagecoach stops. These were

A typical colonial kitchen consisted of a large fireplace that contained a "crane" that moved in and out of the fire and a bake oven that was considered "hot enough" when the hair on a woman's arm singed after being held inside. *Courtesy of Pennsbury Manor, administered by the Pennsylvania Historical and Museum Commission.*

normally more elegant than the other inns, and provided exceptional food and more comfortable sleeping accommodations. As a rule, these inns didn't accept wagoners or drovers, and the rooms in these establishments were larger, with fine furnishings and softer bedding. They housed a formal parlor for family use and private elegant dining facilities for wealthier patrons. These innkeepers courted stagecoach drivers since it was the drivers who decided where to stop the coach, and the rivalry could be intense, not only for the income from the stagecoach operators but for the revenue for food and beverages from the passengers.

Stagecoach stops were named after more prestigious taverns or well-known people in England, such as the King George Inn and the Red Lion Tavern, although during the Revolution some proprietors changed the names of their businesses to reflect the new patriotism of the rebelling nation.

Wagoners and teamsters drove freight wagons that transported agricultural products such as flour and grain to Philadelphia, Trenton and Pittsburgh. The wagon of choice in the early years was the Conestoga, which could carry up to ten tons of freight. Their shape prevented cargo from shifting on uneven terrain, and wagons could be pulled by as many as eight horses. The drivers would travel an average of fifteen miles a day.

A room on the upper floors of a stagecoach hotel was normally more elegantly appointed than those of a wagoner or drover tavern inn. *Courtesy of Langhorne Historic Association.*

After long, hard days on the road, wagoners sought refuge at stands that were operated with them in mind. These taverns didn't have the elegance of the stagecoach stops, but instead catered to men who would end a day on the road by drinking hard, playing cards and if there was any energy left in them, picking a good fistfight. The wagoner carried his own bedroll and blanket and spent the night sleeping on the ground next to his wagon, unless he collapsed on the barroom floor, in which case he was left for the night. (Although before that could happen, the proprietor might be heard telling a patron to mind his p's and q's, since the liquor was dispensed in tankards holding either pints or quarts.)

Drove stands accommodated men who herded livestock along the highways, and they offered corrals and pens for the animals being driven to market. Operators of drove stands made more of a living by selling alcoholic beverages than sleeping quarters.

The least respected of the taverns were the taprooms, which were usually located on the outskirts of town. They were loud, boisterous places, often run by men who made questionable brew that was strong, though not always the best tasting.

Serving ale was common not only in taverns, but in all households. It was a staple in every home at that time since water could be contaminated and cause dysentery. Beer, cider and other relatively weak fermented beverages were generally consumed in America. Even young children drank beer—although it was usually the weakest of the brew. Milk at that time wasn't considered appropriate for human consumption. It

With the introduction of Conestoga wagons, colonists could carry up to eight tons of freight. The shape prevented cargo from shifting on uneven terrain. *Author Collection.*

Colonists brewed their own ale whenever possible and even built separate buildings to accommodate the chore. Ingredients came from their gardens and farms. Even children were given the weakest of the brew to drink. *Courtesy of Pennsbury Manor, administered by the Pennsylvania Historical and Museum Commission.*

was used for cream and to make butter, and the "refuse" was either given to the farm animals or thrown away.

The Art of Brewing Ale in the Seventeenth Century

Beer is the result of the slow fermentation of malted and hopped liquid. It is divided into three basic categories: stout, which is a dark heavy beverage with a high alcoholic content; lager, which is produced by yeast and activated at a relatively low temperature and the lightest form; and ale, somewhere in between the other categories, and is produced by yeast and ferments at around sixty degrees Fahrenheit. Ale was the brew of choice in colonial times because it was produced at a temperature that was easily maintained.

The ingredients included water, preferably water that has a pleasant taste, boiled to destroy any dangerous bacteria that might be present, grain—usually barley, but corn, oats, wheat and rye were also used—and it had to be malted (dried in kilns); molasses or honey to provide nourishment to the yeast, and hops, which are the fruit of a vine-like plant related to the mulberry tree, which gave the ale its characteristic scent and flavor.

The malt was soaked in a large wooden mash tub at low temperatures then separated out of the liquid. The liquid that was left, called "wort," was transferred to a large copper pot. Hops and the other ingredients were then added, and the mixture was boiled for several hours. It was cooled to about seventy degrees and yeast was sprinkled on the mixture. It was stirred periodically with straw that had been tied together and dipped in yeast to quicken the action. When it was fermented, the beverage could be consumed immediately, or stored in barrels.[10]

Stagecoach passengers ate their meals at taverns and inns along the route starting at six o'clock in the morning, with midday meals at around two o'clock in the afternoon and supper at seven o'clock in the evening. *Author Collection.*

In addition to ale and beer, beverages such as gin, rum, whiskey and cider were plentiful at taverns in the colonies, and contrary to what many people think, hard liquor was consumed by all classes. In fact, rum was actually thought to be an excellent remedy for illness. Even Quaker communities allowed the use of good New England or Jamaican rum in the early years of the colony.

Wine and brandy were less available and reserved more for the stagecoach clientele, as were tea and coffee, which were costly and rare. Although hot chocolate was a favorite of William Penn and was served at Pennsbury whenever he was in residence, it was an expensive import and was served only in the most affluent of taverns. A beverage called flip was also served in Pennsylvania taverns, although it was more popular in the New England colonies. Most flips consisted of strong ale or beer with molasses or sugar, dried pumpkin and rum for flavor, although this recipe could change depending upon the preparer. A hot poker—which was also called a loggerhead or flip dog—was plunged into the brew just before serving and gave the beverage a slightly burnt flavor.

Tavern Fare

Breakfasts at the inns were usually served early in the day. In most cases the early meals were as hearty as dinner in order to provide enough nourishment to guests so that they could face long, hard travel on the stagecoach until they reached their destination or the next stop in their journey. Travel by stagecoach was difficult. The coach was a heavy, cumbersome carriage, often without any form of springs, pulled by as many as six horses. They varied in size, but normally up to eight or more affluent passengers could be seated inside a coach. Second-class seats were sometimes available in a large open basket attached to the back, and the least privileged passengers sat on the roof with the luggage, holding on to a handrail for dear life to keep from being thrown off on the rough, bumpy roads of colonial America. The sides of the carriage were wood, and curtains made of leather, which could be rolled open to allow for ventilation in the warmer months, did very little to keep passengers dry on rainy days or warm in cold temperatures.

First developed in the British Isles in the 1500s, stagecoaches in colonial America were considerably less elegant and traveled over rougher roads than their counterparts in Europe. An especially slow mode of transportation, the stagecoach traveled an average of about four miles an hour and it was customary for stage drivers to stop every ten or twelve miles to rest or change horses and give the passengers time to eat and enjoy a brief respite. Since stagecoach drivers were determined to keep to their schedule, passengers rushed through their meals, and if they were late getting to the table they went hungry until the next meal, which was usually around two o'clock in the afternoon, followed by supper at seven o'clock.

The food at most taverns was inexpensive and abundant. Menus included meats and vegetables that were available according to the season. Beef, ham, salt pork, bacon, mutton, squirrel, venison and wild turkey were usual fare, but a meal could also include

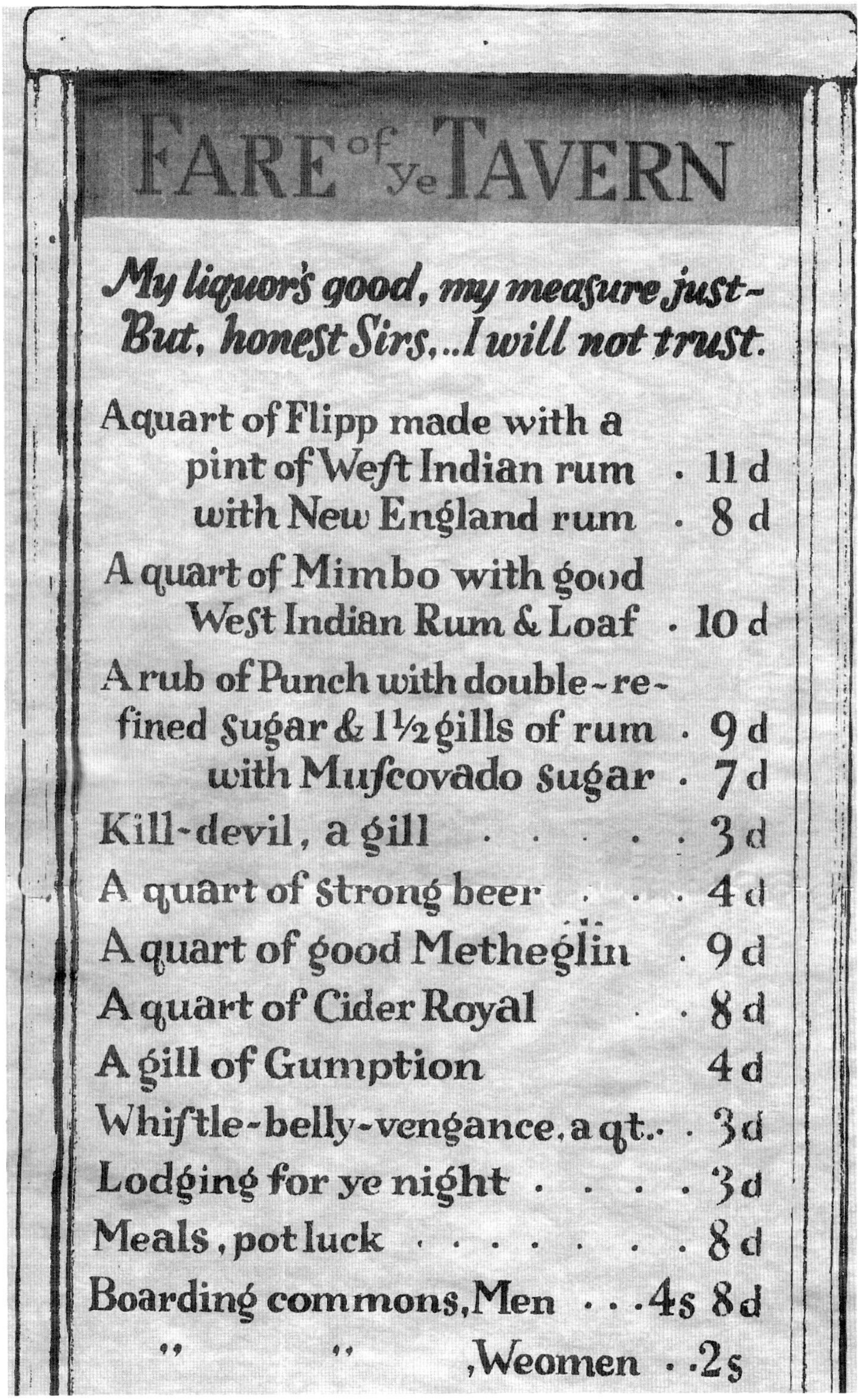

Most taverns exhibited their fees on the wall behind the bar, and prompt payment was usually mandatory. *Courtesy of Historical Documents, Inc.*

bear steaks, quail, pheasant and fish indigenous to the region, such as shad, trout, catfish and salmon. Cheeses and bread, or biscuits, were served with the meats, as well as johnnycakes, corn pone and buckwheat cakes. Molasses and honey were used as sweeteners, and herbs, such as marjoram, parsley, dill and thyme, were used generously for seasoning. The apple, with all its variations such as apple butter and cider, was a staple. A tavern's garden—indeed every household garden—was vital in keeping people fed and nourished. Whatever vegetables and fruits were available in the winter and early spring depended upon how talented the woman of the house or tavern was in preserving the excess produce from her gardens during the harvest.

Colonists used several methods of preserving and storing food. Fresh cuts of meat were packed in coarse salt for several weeks, which drew fluid from the flesh. Then the meat was hung in a wooden shed that had no flue or windows called a smokehouse or meat house. A fire would burn slowly for one or two weeks to further dry the meat. Meats preserved this way might last for months or even years before being eaten. If there was room, the meats were hung in the subterranean room of the tavern so that they weren't smoked more than necessary. Unfortunately, when the tavern keeper or cook went to get the meat deep into the winter months, uninvited guests, such as rats or other rodents, may have already feasted on the dinner that was to be served in the dining room upstairs.

Travelers at the inn ate their food on either pewter or wooden plates, and flatware was made of pewter or wood, although the horns of animals were often carved in shapes for this purpose, closely resembling modern plastic that we use today. Fine silver and china were rarely found in public houses—or in most homes for that matter—during the seventeenth or eighteenth centuries.

TAVERN SIGNS

Whether a tavern was a stagecoach stop, a taproom or accommodated the wagoner or drover, it provided refuge from hard work, exhausting travel or the problems of the day. It was a place to rest or to exchange news, hear politicians speak or see justice take place. It was the center of the community. And befitting that importance, it was identified by a sign that was often a stunning work of art.

Red lions, raging bulls, flying eagles, high-stepping stallions, stately trees and birds in the palm of a hand hung in public exhibition as America's first billboards. In addition to heralding ale, food and lodging, the tavern and inn signs proved to be excellent landmarks long before street signs were invented. When a traveler needed directions, the answer would inevitably contain the words: "When you reach the sign of the...."

The establishment of Bucks County roads opened travel and trade in every direction and new turnpikes meant more traffic, so the number of inns grew as well. When the canal along the Delaware River connecting Easton to Philadelphia was built, even more taverns and inns were needed to offer refreshment and lodging to the men who drove the mules, steered the boats and operated the canals. Decorative signs sprung up at almost every crossroad, alongside the canal and at ferry stops.

Outbuildings at most taverns included smokehouses, icehouses, stables and "necessaries." Smokehouses prevented meat from spoiling, and hanging the meat kept rodents from eating it. *Courtesy of Pennsbury Manor, administered by the Pennsylvania Historical and Museum Commission.*

Many of the signs conveyed important information about the town, the political climate or indicated whether the tavern was a stagecoach stop or welcomed drovers and wagon drivers. In fact, the paintings on the signs might even be used to convey surreptitious meanings, such as whether a Patriot or a Tory would be welcomed inside. During the American Revolution, taverns would be occupied by either Patriots or Tories—but rarely ever by both at the same time.

Creating a tavern sign was a team effort in most cases. A joiner, or woodworker, would design the wooden shape, which could be oval, rectangular, horizontal or vertical. A blacksmith would be needed to form the hanging iron hardware, which was sometimes attached to the building over the door of the taproom or freestanding by the side of the road. A painter put the finishing touch on the wood, designing the picture or lettering at the suggestion of the innkeeper, generally using brilliant paints. For the more elaborate tavern or stagecoach inn, wood carving and turning was used along with decorative and intricate ironwork. Ground glass was sometimes added to catch the light and draw a passerby's eye to the sign—which could be very valuable in areas heavily populated with taverns or where several stagecoach inns competed with one another.

Utensils made of animal horns (inset) and gourds hollowed out and dried were commonly used for eating and for serving. *Courtesy of Pennsbury Manor, administered by the Pennsylvania Historical and Museum Commission.*

The styles of signs changed with each generation and as more colonists learned to read and write, lettering became more prominent and horizontal signs became more prevalent in order to accommodate the lettering. Lettering in signs produced in the 1800s overshadowed the symbol of the animal or bird that may have been used in earlier years, and often the picture was completely omitted to leave room for sophisticated and gilded lettering and adornment.

White pine was the wood of choice for tavern signs as it was plentiful, easy to carve and durable. Linseed oil and shellac mixed with calcium carbonate were used to increase the pine wood's tolerance to the outdoors, yet exposure to the elements often faded the paints and it wasn't unusual for signs to be painted over, either replicating the original artwork or completely replacing it with a different design, name or message. Before the Revolution, typical signs mirrored those in Britain or showed the likeness of popular military figures from England. During and after the Revolution, these signs were painted over to reflect American patriotism and liberation, as well as the great military heroes of the American War for Independence.

Pennsylvania is said to have had more inns and taverns than any other colony. This is not surprising since Philadelphia became the largest city next to London under British rule. In 1744 there were thirty licensed taverns and inns in Bucks County alone and by 1830 there were 128.[11]

Decorative signs weren't only used outside, but often decorated the walls of the rooms inside, and the signboards usually had something to do with the danger of not paying promptly. One sign in a tavern in Durham Township illustrated a dead dog with its feet sticking straight up in the air. Beneath the picture, the inscription read: "Old Trust is dead, bad pay killed him."

Tavern signs sprung up at every crossroad and ferry stop as roads expanded and villages were established. The signs were used as road directions, political statements and works of art. *Half Moon sign at the Court Inn, Courtesy of Newtown Historical Society.*

Several of America's renowned folk artists and portraitists began their careers as sign painters or were forced to paint signs to make ends meet and pay the bills when necessary; however, the trade was so common that many others disappeared into anonymity, although their creations are still displayed and admired either by individual collectors or in museums.

Among the most illustrious of sign painters is Benjamin West, who was a friend of Benjamin Franklin. As a child he had learned how to make paint from Native Americans, and from that time he worked hard to develop his skill. He left America when he was a young man to live and study in Italy and London, and he became an illustrious portraitist after painting images of several members of the royal family while there, including several of King George III. He married Elizabeth Shewell, a Philadelphia socialite, but not without intrigue and great machinations on the part of several famous figures of that time, including Benjamin Franklin (See Pen Ryn in Chapter 4). Another sign painter, Gilbert Charles Stuart, was born in Rhode Island and moved to London to study under Benjamin West. Upon his return to the newly formed United States, he set up a studio in Philadelphia and painted a series of portraits of George Washington and other political leaders of that time. In fact, one of his images of Washington remains on the dollar bill to this day.

Known mostly for his *Peaceable Kingdom* paintings, Edward Hicks was a native son of Bucks County, and was born in 1780 to Isaac and Catherine Hicks. His grandfather, Gilbert, a wealthy businessman and substantial landowner in Bucks County, was regarded as a traitor at the outbreak of the Revolutionary War because of his affiliations with the Crown. The family's lands were confiscated and Gilbert fled to England.

Edward's parents remained in the United States, but were forced to live less affluently than they had before the war. Then Catherine died and Isaac, unable to care for his young children alone and without the financial means to hire someone to assist him, boarded his children with several Bucks County families. Edward, who was the youngest of the Hicks children and only two years old, went to live with a Quaker family named Twining on their farm in Newtown. He was especially fond of his foster mother, Elizabeth Twining, and flourished under her compassionate care. Although not born Quaker, Edward was deeply influenced by the faith of his foster family during the years in which he lived on the Twining farm.

When he was nearly thirteen years of age, he began an apprenticeship with coach makers Henry and William Tomlinson, whose business was located in Four Lanes End (Langhorne). He spent five years learning the business, but seemed most adept at the ornamental painting that adorned the doors and trim. When his apprenticeship ended, Edward went to work as a junior partner with Joshua C. Canby, a coach maker in the neighboring town of Milford, now known as Hulmeville. He remained there from 1801 until 1811. During that time, he met and married Sarah Worstall, a member of the Society of Friends, and he embraced the faith to which he had been so drawn as a child. He was received into membership at the Middletown Monthly Meeting. His increasing work for the Friends became the most important aspect of his life, and in 1811 Hicks became a Quaker minister, and went into his own business as a decorative painter of carriages, furniture, clock faces and elaborate signs.

A tavern sign painted by Edward Hicks ca.1830s depicting Penn's treaty with the American Indians is in safekeeping at the Newtown Historical Society. *Courtesy of Newtown Historical Society.*

Unfortunately, his art was frowned upon by his fellow Quakers as frivolous and contrary to their "plain" way of living. Recognizing that his ornamental painting was in conflict with his faith, he gave it up reluctantly. As a Quaker minister, he traveled extensively, preaching throughout Eastern Pennsylvania, Delaware and New Jersey; however, Quaker ministers weren't paid and he fell deeply into debt. Painting was the only way he knew to support his family, and so the Friends in his congregation agreed to allow him to paint within the bounds of their belief in living a plain and simple existence.

Ultimately it was the profound influence of his religious life that led him to create the *Peaceable Kingdom* pictures for which he is known today. In this work, he depicted Isaiah 11:6. In subsequent paintings that are sometimes called the "border" Kingdoms, he

Peaceable Kingdom by Edward Hicks ca.1830s. *Courtesy of Newtown Historical Society.*

lettered the words of the passage around the edge of the panel: "The wolf shall also dwell with the lamb, and the leopard shall lie down with the kid; and the calf and the young lion and the fatling together; and a little child shall lead them."

Calling his renditions *The Peaceable Kingdom of the Branch,* Hicks felt that through this form of art he was providing images consistent with Quaker beliefs. He painted *Peaceable Kingdom* panels and canvases, as well as other religious and historical images, until his death in 1849.

A chair painted by Edward Hicks is displayed in the Newtown Historic Library, and two of his paintings can be seen in the James A. Michener Art Museum in Doylestown.

Part II

From Tyranny to Liberty…
Colony to Commonwealth

Author Collection.

Chapter 3

Patriots, Tories and War

One flag, one land, one heart, one hand and one nation evermore!
—American Patriot Toast

Perhaps the most notable and certainly the most legendary role that Bucks County played in the Revolutionary War was hosting General George Washington and his Continental Army during the days leading up to and following Christmas 1776. It was in Bucks County that Washington planned one of his most strategic moves in the war and gathered his troops to cross the frozen Delaware River to converge in an attack on the Hessian soldiers in the Battle of Trenton—a decision that proved him to be a true military genius.

During the years leading up to the Revolutionary War, the residents of Bucks County focused primarily on settling the land, building their farms and finding ways in which to transport their produce and other goods for trade.

Then, when George III became king of England in 1760 and levied a series of taxes against the colonists in an effort to recoup money lost during the French and Indian War, Pennsylvanians turned their attention to the New England colonists' rumblings against new taxes that they declared to be unfair. New England colonies were at first annoyed by the control the king was asserting over them, then they became enraged when he issued the Stamp Act of 1765, which required that stamps be purchased from Britain for all newspapers and legal documents. The Townshend Acts of 1767 imposed new taxes on glass, paper, teas, paints and other goods shipped to the colonies from Britain. Tensions between the colonies and Britain grew steadily as Britain restricted colonists from competing with British businesses and prevented American colonists from selling their goods to countries other than Britain, even when the country was willing to pay a higher price than the English. In 1765, the *Boston Gazette* wrote:

> *A colonist cannot make a button, a horseshoe, nor a hobnail, but some snooty ironmonger or respectable buttonmaker of England shall bawl and squall that his honor's worship is most egregiously maltreated, injured, cheated, and robbed by the rascally American republicans.*[12]

Additionally, the British refused to allow the colonies government representation in Parliament, believing that their own appointed government officials adequately represented the colonies. As a result, growing resentment pushed the colonies to create their own laws and ignore the British laws they resented.

New England was the first area of the New World to express displeasure with the king's policies, and Boston drew up a statement of rights and grievances and sent them to colonists throughout Massachusetts. In time, these grievances were adopted by all the New England colonies. Then the Virginia Assembly appointed a standing committee of correspondence similar to Massachusetts's and encouraged other colonies to do the same. By 1774, a network of committees of correspondence was established representing the libertarian sentiments of all of the colonies.

Before this time, colonists had been satisfied subjects of the British Crown; they were content as long as they enjoyed the same constitutional rights and civil liberties as Englishmen in England, and prior to 1775 there was very little overt sentiment concerning American patriotism versus loyalty to England. But now colonists strongly objected to taxation without representation.

New roads began to connect the colonies, and better communication between cities and settlements was established. The colonies began to feel an alliance with each other and divisiveness toward Britain. Yet colonists were split on the subject of independence, and both rich and poor argued on both sides of the issue. In Pennsylvania, the large Quaker population was against any violence that would result from the quest for separation from Britain. Taking up arms was utterly contradictory to their precepts.

However, when Britain closed Boston Harbor through the Boston Port Act in 1774 in an effort to squelch the rebellious actions of Massachusetts residents, the Pennsylvania Committee of Correspondence announced its support for the besieged Bostonians. On July 9, 1774, Bucks County residents supported the idea of forming a general congress to represent all the colonies and sent seven representatives to the provincial convention.

The First Continental Congress met at Carpenter's Hall in Philadelphia in September 1774 and the following December issued a document known as the Articles of Association of 1774, which recommended that the colonies unite to oppose England's unjust taxes. In January 1775 another convention was held in order to approve a boycott against importing British goods to the colonies as called for in the Articles. Every county and town was urged to create a committee to enforce the boycott.

The Bucks County Committee of Safety was elected on December 15, 1774, but its members were a conservative delegation and refused to attend this important convention because they believed it was too radical. Pennsylvania fared better than other colonies with the British Crown, and thanks to William Penn's "Holy Experiment" the colony's constitution was more liberal than most. Many Pennsylvanians were reluctant to separate from England.

Bucks County's attitude changed when it learned of the battles at Lexington and Concord in the spring of 1775. Realizing that war was on the horizon, the committee of safety recommended that the county form a military association and that its residents prepare themselves to take up arms to aid their country in the fight for independence.

The Bucks County Military Association was made up of three battalions representing the lower, middle and upper regions.

Many of the English and German pacifist sects living in Bucks were torn over the issue of independence, and it began to divide their own communities. Because of their strong convictions, they were treated with hostility and suspicion for the first time in a colony that was set up under William Penn to provide them with a safe place to practice their faith according to their own consciences. Some Quakers broke away from the Society of Friends because of their strong patriotic sentiment. Quaker Joseph Kirkbride, who was born in Falls Township in 1731, was one of Bucks County's most active revolutionaries and a colonel in the First Battalion of Bucks County Military Association.

There also was a large contingent of British loyalists in the county. Called Tories, many were large landowners who held political positions and felt they had much to lose if the colonists proceeded to fight for independence. Although it is easy today to look back at these residents of Bucks County—indeed all colonists like them—as traitors to the "cause," we must also consider that these men were not as much traitors to a country that had not yet been formed as they were loyal to the country and its sovereign of which they had always been part. To them England was their country; King George III was their king. And so several took up arms for the British and formed military groups such as the Bucks County Light Dragoons and the Bucks County Volunteers, and individuals such as the Doan brothers made certain others knew where they stood. Other Tories were secretive about their loyalty to the Crown and provided shelter and provisions to the British Army through surreptitious movements.

Joseph Galloway was an elected and influential member of the provincial assembly who lived in Trevose in Bensalem Township. He was a very close friend of Benjamin Franklin, and served as a Bucks County justice in the courts at Newtown. He was a powerful force in Pennsylvania politics at that time, and he was strongly opposed to severing ties with England. As a representative to the Continental Congress, he worked diligently for peaceful solutions with England, but when his efforts failed, he felt he had no choice but to join the Royalists in Philadelphia. Although he served as an advisor to General Lord William Howe, he would not take up arms against his fellow countrymen. Galloway was not the only official in Bucks County to remain loyal to England. He was joined by Judge Gilbert Hicks of Langhorne and Sheriff William Biles. Their neighbors and friends were now their enemies, and they must have been deeply troubled when they followed their own consciences to remain loyal to the Crown even though in their hearts they were Americans.

The committee of safety was to report that in Bucks County there were 1,688 sympathizers for the war for independence and 1,613 did not support the idea of independence. Nearly half of Bucks County residents were Loyalists.[13]

The Bucks County Committee of Observation, which met at the White Bear Tavern (later called the Spread Eagle Inn) was charged with investigating, reprimanding or prosecuting any dissenters, and according to the numbers mentioned above, they were kept busy. A resolution was passed to seize and sell the property of all residents who aided the British or joined the British Army. All dissenters were subjected to additional taxes for resisting military service, and laws were passed requiring them to swear oaths of allegiance and to bear arms. They were allowed, however, to pay others to fight on their behalf.

Governor John Penn and the Pennsylvania Assembly remained opposed to the Revolution and they refused to allow the colonists to determine the course their government should pursue. As a result, the Philadelphia Committee of Safety renounced the Pennsylvania Assembly's authority and called for a convention to establish a new government. This time, the Bucks County delegates attended, and at this convention, which was held in June 1776, they agreed that a new Pennsylvania constitution was necessary. They also concurred that voting qualifications should be determined to ensure fair representation of the colony's population, and they supported the proposed Declaration of Independence. One Bucks Countian signed the document.

George Taylor was born in Ireland, the son of a clergyman, and although very well educated, he had been an indentured servant upon arriving in the colonies. His employer was a man named Savage, and Taylor worked under his direction first as an ironworker and then in Savage's office as a clerk. Upon the death of Savage, he married the Widow Savage and became proprietor of the Durham Iron Works and his wealth grew. Although it had not been his intention to enter into politics, he was elected to the provincial assembly in 1764, and was a member of the committee of correspondence and the committee of safety. On July 20, 1776, after the initial reading of the Declaration, the Pennsylvania convention chose new representatives. Those members who had opposed the Declaration of Independence were not reelected. George Taylor was one of the newly elected and signed the final copy on August 2.

Other signers of the Declaration of Independence moved to Bucks County during and after the war. Robert Morris, who has been called the financier of the American Revolution, purchased the Summerseat property, 2,500 acres along the Delaware. He was appointed superintendent of finance for the United States, established the Bank of North America and was a member of the United States Senate. It had been his hope that Summerseat would become the capital of the United States, but George Washington had other ideas. Eventually, Morris's land speculations in New York led to severe financial reverses. In the end, the man who "financed" the war for liberty in the New World was sent to debtor's prison in Philadelphia. George Clymer, another signer of the Declaration of Independence, purchased Summerseat from Morris and lived there until his death in 1813.

Now the colonies were at war with England, and Bucks County was a source of valuable commodities in the Revolution. The committee of observation assumed responsibility for ensuring that all imperative war commodities, such as coal, sulfur, iron ore and saltpeter, were available to the owners of the county's gunpowder mills. The Durham Furnace in the upper portion of the county provided the army with shot and shells, while Bucks County farms provided food—in many cases for both the Continental and the British armies when they were camped in the Delaware Valley. Saltpeter was manufactured in the county and several powder mills were established.

In early December 1776 the Continental Army was greatly challenged, and George Washington's troops arrived in Bucks County tired, ragged and counting the days until they could leave their commission at the end of the month. General Washington was greatly troubled by the way the American Revolution was playing out. Since August, the Americans had been chased relentlessly by the British and Hessians from Long Island and Manhattan across New Jersey, losing one battle after another.

Washington knew the British planned to march into the capital city of Philadelphia by sweeping the American Army aside. When the American troops crossed the Delaware River into Pennsylvania in December, Washington ordered all the boats along the New Jersey side of the Delaware confiscated, including the large Durham boats, and all smaller boats destroyed. Then he had the boats hidden behind two islands on the Pennsylvania side of the Delaware to prevent the British and Hessians from crossing the Delaware. This would give his men time to rest and Washington and his officers a chance to regroup and strategize their next move.

At this point in the war, the British were confident that the Revolution had been crushed, and General Washington wasn't certain they were wrong. The British had outmaneuvered the Continental Army numerous times and the series of defeats left the American troops demoralized and in despair. The morale of the soldiers was at an all- time low. To make matters worse, most of them were fighting in tattered clothing, many without boots or shoes. They marched with rags wrapped around their feet during what was a harsh and unforgiving winter.

When they arrived in Pennsylvania, Washington had five thousand men; seventeen hundred of them needed medical attention due to disease, wounds or as a result of the harsh weather. During earlier retreats, Washington had lost important supplies and many of his men had deserted. He also lost contact with two divisions of his army. Additionally, enlistments of the militias under his command were due to expire at the end of the month, and Washington sensed that many would not reenlist. He sent out orders to recruit men and to gather supplies. His first concern was to feed and care for the troops; then he needed to find a way to renew their commitment to the war.

Major General Charles Lee's division of two thousand men arrived at camp—without General Lee, for he had been captured by the British when he had taken refuge in a small tavern in Basking Ridge, New Jersey. When Lee's division was followed by General Horatio Gates's division of five hundred men and Colonel John Cadwalader's one thousand men, morale in camp picked up slightly. With these reinforcements, and a small number of new volunteers from Bucks County, Washington now had six thousand able-bodied men.

Washington and his officers took up residence in private homes and inns throughout Bucks County. Washington first made his headquarters at Summerseat in Morrisville. General William Alexander took up residence at the Thompson-Neely house in Upper Makefield, where a makeshift hospital had been set up for the troops. General Nathanael Greene used Bogart's Tavern in Buckingham (the Merrick House), and the rest stayed in homes located mostly along the Delaware from Bristol to Coryell's Ferry (New Hope) and points north. The troops camped on the frozen farmland around these homes and taverns, wherever officers could reach their troops without difficulty.

Bogart's Tavern was the headquarters of the committee of observation in Bucks County and General Nathanael Greene's quarters in December 1776. *Author Collection.*

From December 7 until Christmas Day, Washington and his officers met at each other's headquarters and in local taverns to organize their next move against the British. It was imperative for the morale of the troops to accomplish a victory before their commissions were up, and he planned a daring attack against the Hessian garrison in Trenton. Thirty thousand Hessian soldiers from Germany had been "hired" by King George III to assist his army in the American war. The Hessian Army was well trained and had fought beside British troops during the Seven Years' War and other British conflicts. Called mercenaries because of the financial arrangement with Britain to fight in the colonies, they had a reputation for being brutish in their treatment of the colonists in every town they controlled, and the Continental Army knew they were formidable opponents. Approximately fourteen hundred Hessians were at Trenton that December.

Washington's plan called for his men to cross from McKonkey's Ferry in Upper Makefield, while Lieutenant Colonel John Cadwalader would cross at Dunk's Ferry in Bristol and Brigadier General James Ewing would cross at Trenton Ferry. Knowing that he was in equally divided territory between Patriots and Loyalists, Washington and his officers were careful to keep their plans as secretive as possible, moving from one headquarters to another and meeting quietly wherever they thought it was safe, certain that there could be Tory spies among the Bucks Countians who served them food and ale.

On December 23 Washington ordered that each man be provided with three days rations and that they keep their blankets handy, but they were given no further orders except for the password of the day, "Victory or Death," which General Washington himself wrote out on small pieces of paper. Security was tightened at all the river crossings in fear that the British and Hessians would learn of his plans. The Durham boats hidden at Malta Island were brought closer to the ferry landings where three columns of militia would cross the river and rendezvous on the march to Trenton. All the extra ferries along the Delaware were commanded to be brought to McKonkey's, Dunk's and Trenton's Ferries.

That December, the author Thomas Paine—famous for his pamphlet *Common Sense*, which had served to increase support for the Revolution in its early days—published *The American Crisis*. The release of this new pamphlet was in perfect timing with Washington's plans, and the document was read aloud to the troops. It began with the words, "These are the times that try men's souls…Tyranny, like hell, is not easily conquered; yet we have this consolation with us, that the harder the conflict, the more glorious the triumph."[14]

Washington's Continental Army was about to face a night and a day that would certainly try their souls and their physical strength. On Christmas Eve, Washington spent the day and night with General Green at Merrick's Bogart Tavern. The Merrick family was sent to a neighbor's home that night so that the council of generals could speak without worry of being overheard. The next day he arrived at McKonkey's Ferry Inn, and along with some of his closest advisors and general officers, he sat in the main dining room making final details for the battle that would become known as a turning point for the Continental Army in the war for independence.

After delegating responsibilities to several large groups of the militia to guard the ferries between Bristol and Coryell's Ferry, and to protect supplies in Newtown and the sick and wounded who would be left behind in Bucks County, Washington gathered 2,400 men near the cove where the boats were hidden. His officers would include Greene, Mercer, Sterling, Stephen, Sullivan, Knox, Hand, Monroe, Hamilton, Ewing and Cadwalader.

Although Christmas Day dawned clear, by evening the weather was stormy and sleet and snow pelted the ground. Washington and his officers ate Christmas dinner in McKonkey's Ferry Tavern and watched the nor'easter grow uglier by the hour. Some of his officers doubted the crossing was possible in such turbulent conditions. In spite of the weather, at around six o'clock in the evening while sitting in the tavern Washington wrote a message to Colonel Cadwalader in Bristol saying: "I am determined, as the night is favorable to cross the River, to make the attack upon Trenton in the morning. If you can do nothing real, at least create as great a diversion as possible."[15]

It was Washington's intention to have his army on the other side of the river by midnight, but due to the unfavorable conditions the crossing dragged on all night. Hundreds of men located at McKonkey's Ferry alone were loaded into no more than thirty boats throughout the night. The boats were rowed across a raging river filled with ice floes, which clung to the sides of the boats and had to be pushed off by the shivering men.

In 1776, McKonkey's Ferry Tavern was just a small three-story building with an underground kitchen, a barroom, formal dining room and two sleeping rooms upstairs. *Courtesy Washington Crossing Historic Park, administered by the Pennsylvania Historical and Museum Commission.*

General Washington ate his Christmas dinner in the McKonkey's Ferry Tavern before crossing the Delaware during a frigid nor'easter. *Courtesy Washington Crossing Historic Park, administered by the Pennsylvania Historical and Museum Commission.*

In the meantime, artillery officer Colonel Henry Knox, who had been instrumental in saving Boston from the British when he transported fifty-five pieces of artillery from Fort Ticonderoga in New York earlier in the year, oversaw the transportation of the horses and artillery across the river by ferry. He knew the troops would not move forward until the artillery was with them.

Colonel Knox's booming voice was invaluable that night considering he had to be heard over the roar of the wind from the nor'easter and the noise of the rushing waters of the river. Sleet and snow stung his face as he stood at the edge of the ferry shouting orders and scrutinizing the soldiers under his command as they struggled against the weather to load the ferries and boats.

Knox was responsible for eighteen fieldpieces, including various sized cannons. The standard rule of thumb for firepower per troop at that time was two to three guns per one thousand muskets, but for the Battle of Trenton, there was one cannon for approximately every 130 men, giving Washington's troops an advantage.

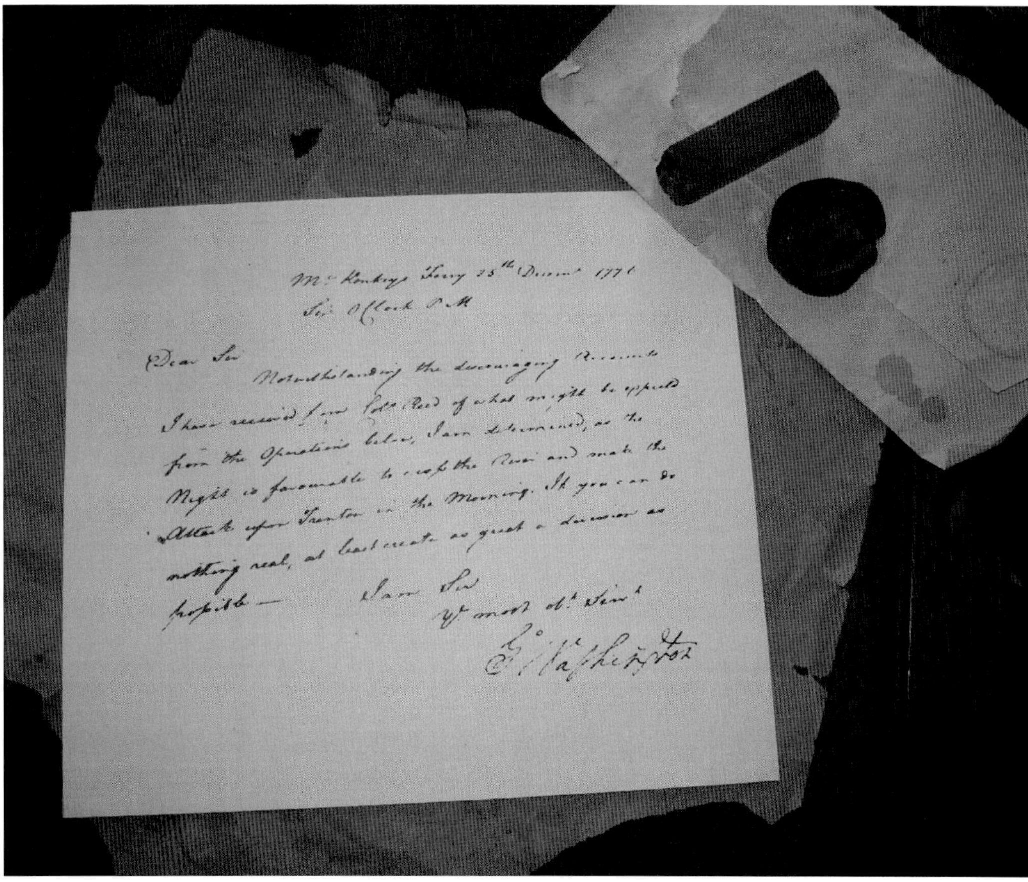

McKonkey's Ferry 25th Decem 1776
Six O'Clock P.M.

Dear Sir
Notwithstanding the discouraging accounts I have received from Coll Reed of what might be expected from the Operations below, I am determined, as the Night is favourable to cross the River and make the attack upon Trenton in the Morning. If you can do nothing real, at least create as great a diversion as possible —
I am Sir
Yr most obt Servt
G^o Washington

General Washington wrote a note to General Greene stating, "I am determined...to make an attack upon Trenton in the morning." *Courtesy Washington Crossing Historic Park, administered by the Pennsylvania Historical and Museum Commission.*

Getting the artillery across the Delaware River in what could easily be considered the worst of circumstances was no easy task, but Knox was as determined to put his armaments in place as Washington was his militia. Washington's confidence in Knox was well founded, and he was the only officer of the artillery that night that completed the task. Knox was to later write to his wife: "Perseverance accomplished what at first seemed impossible."[16]

Cadwalader was facing the same conditions at Dunk's Ferry, and although he was able to get his troops to the other side, they could not accomplish what Knox had with the artillery. Without the weapons that were imperative in a successful campaign, Cadwalader recalled his men and they did not join Washington's column for the march on Trenton; nor did Ewing and his men, who never even attempted their crossing from Trenton Ferry.

It took eleven hours for the entire crossing, much longer than Washington had anticipated. Once the artillery was unloaded and in place, the march on Trenton began, albeit critically late. There would be no element of surprise under darkness

The Durham boats were designed to carry cargo on the Delaware to Philadelphia. The largest were sixty-five feet long and eight feet wide and could transport up to twenty tons of iron. *Courtesy Washington Crossing Historic Park, administered by the Pennsylvania Historical and Museum Commission.*

as Washington had intended, but instead by the time the Continental Army reached Trenton it would be daylight.

If the crossing on the Delaware was hard in sleet and snow and raging wind, the march through the same conditions was no easier. The soldiers followed the path by following the drips and smears of blood left by the barefooted soldiers who marched in front of them.

Washington had ordered the army split into two columns, one under his and General Green's command, and one under General Sullivan's. Sullivan's column would follow River Road while Washington's column would follow Pennington Road inland, in this way approaching Trenton on two major roads leading into town.

If Washington was worried about attacking in daylight, his fears were allayed when he realized that the Hessians were still groggy, and some still asleep, after their Christmas celebrations from the night before. The attack at eight o'clock in the morning was successful and complete, with nine hundred Hessians taken prisoner, twenty to thirty killed and the rest fleeing for their lives. By most accounts, no American lives were lost during this battle, though several soldiers were wounded.

Washington and his officers' fear that word about the attack would get to the British and Hessians before the Continental Army reached Trenton, however, was founded. Fortunately, the Hessian commander, Johann Gottleib Rall (sometimes spelled Rahl) had ignored warnings from Tory spies from Bucks County that the Americans would attack, and the price he paid for this ignorance was his life. He died the same day from wounds he received in the battle, the note about the attack still in his pocket, unread.

This successful surprise attack was to prove to the British that the American cause was far from over, and that the desire for liberty burned hotter in the hearts of the patriots than the winter snows and nor'easter winds could extinguish.

Although it was probably tempting for Washington and his officers to consider forging ahead after this victory and continuing to attack and capture outlying enemy posts, he knew that his army was exhausted after the difficult nighttime crossing and freezing march that followed it. After resting in Trenton for a short time, the American army collected their prisoners, gathered the arms and supplies they gained as a result of winning this battle and returned to McKonkey's Ferry on the same boats they had taken in the middle of the night. No doubt there was great celebration at the tavern that night and a very different mood must have permeated the tiny building as Washington and his officers toasted to their victory before moving on to new headquarters in Newtown.

In a letter from Washington to the Continental Congress following this battle, Washington praised his army by stating:

> *In justice to the officers and men, I must add, that their behavior upon this occasion reflects the highest honor upon them. The difficulty of passing the river in a very severe night, and their march through a violent storm of snow and hail, did not in the least abate their ardor; but, when they came to the charge, each seemed to vie with the other in pressing forward and were I to give preference to any particular corps, I should do great injustice to the others.*[17]

The prisoners were taken to Newtown and were quartered in several buildings there. The Hessian officers were taken to the Brick Hotel, then known as the Red Lion Inn, and several others were quartered at the Bird in Hand. The rest were taken to the Presbyterian Church and the jail. Washington entertained several of the officers, while Lord Sterling entertained the rest at the Red Lion Inn. The American Army rested for several days in Bucks County while Washington prepared a second strike. Lord Sterling (William Alexander) had become ill during the crossing and subsequent battle, and had taken up residence at the Justices' House hotel. Knowing that any attacks he would plan would have to be done without Alexander, Washington left him in charge of overseeing whatever prisoners were kept in Newtown, while the rest were moved to other parts of Pennsylvania.

The British anticipated another attack after the American's success in Trenton, and were watching closely from the New Jersey side. At night they kept their eyes on the fires along the Pennsylvania side of the Delaware, thinking that as long as there were fires, the troops were in camp. What they didn't know was that the fires were a decoy to keep them from suspecting a second passage by river.

Washington, this time accompanied by Cadwalader and Ewing, crossed the river again on December 29. They knew that a strong British detachment was now in Trenton, so Washington marched by a back road into Princeton. On the way, they met a battalion of British and some of the American's started to retreat. Washington rode into the fray, his six-foot-one-inch frame high in his saddle, commanding his men to stand their ground and they did, winning the skirmish.

Washington said to his men, "Parade with us, my dear fellows, the day is ours!"[18] They marched on to enjoy another successful engagement against the British in Princeton.

Although General Washington ordered a military hospital be set up in Four Lanes End (Langhorne) and it remained there until the spring of 1777, the Continental Army went into permanent winter quarters at Morristown, New Jersey, after these two infamous victories. The American cause was still alive; the army was intact and their morale lifted by their victories at Trenton and Princeton. Many of the troops reenlisted at the end of the year buoyed by the thrill of their victory, their faith renewed in George Washington. No doubt his offer of a monetary bonus for all who reenlisted helped them to make their decision.

Bucks County continued to play a role in the events of the American Revolution as the war was far from over after the historic crossing on Christmas. Both the British and Continental armies continued to march through the area, sought supplies and exchanged prisoners. General Benedict Arnold was quartered at Coryell's Ferry in the summer of 1777. George Washington made his headquarters at the home of John Moland in Bucks County in 1778. It wasn't until the battles moved to the Southern colonies that a cautious peace came to Bucks County.

The French, reassured by Washington's abilities, provided the Americans with supplies, arms and finally troops, but it wasn't until October 19, 1781, that the British surrendered at Yorktown in Virginia. After the surrender, General Charles Cornwallis, the British commander in chief, said to Washington, "When the illustrious part that

In a reenactment, George Washington addresses his troops on the cold, snowy banks of the Delaware River. Every Christmas Day, people from all over the nation come to witness Washington's Crossing of the Delaware. *Courtesy Washington Crossing Historic Park, administered by the Pennsylvania Historical and Museum Commission.*

your Excellency has borne in this long and arduous contest becomes a matter of history, fame will gather your brightest laurels rather from the banks of the Delaware than from those of the Chesapeake."[19]

McKonkey's Ferry Tavern remained a center of the community, as did most of the ferry crossings along the Delaware. The village of Taylorsville grew around McKonkey's Ferry and ownership of the tavern changed from Samuel McKonkey to Benjamin Taylor in 1777. The tavern was expanded with another taproom and parlor, and a new kitchen was added on the first floor. Benjamin's sons continued to develop the village, first by constructing their own homes, one of which is now a restaurant called the Washington Crossing Inn, and then by building several smaller homes that attracted crafters and artisans. Where once only Samuel McKonkey's ferry and tavern occupied the landscape, an entire village grew and became one of the most vital areas in Bucks County.

McKonkey's Ferry Tavern and several of the buildings in Taylorsville that were erected in the eighteenth century are now part of Washington Crossing Historic Park and have been painstakingly preserved. Tours are given regularly, and it is an inspiring experience to stand in the room where General George Washington and his courageous officers ate their Christmas dinner while making their final plans for what was to become one of the greatest victories of the Revolutionary War.

After the War for Independence was over, 17,000 Hessians returned to Germany, 7,700 died either from wounds sustained in battle or from disease, and approximately five thousand remained in America and became farmers or craftsmen.[20]

King George III

King George III was determined to keep fighting even after the surrender at Yorktown, and he abdicated the throne when Parliament refused to continue to fight but quickly rescinded his abdication. He comforted himself by thinking that George Washington would become a dictator and the Americans would long to be under the security of the Crown once again. He was shocked when he was told that Washington had intended to resign his commission. The king was to have the "satisfaction" of fighting the American's once more when the newly formed country declared war against Britain in 1812. During all of this time, the king was not well. He suffered from a hereditary disease called porphyria, which had been passed down to him from Mary Queen of Scots. In addition to many other symptoms, the disease causes the interruption of nerve impulses to the brain that often results in the development of psychiatric symptoms. George III had been suffering with the effects of the disease for ten years prior to the American's Declaration for Independence, and by 1811 it was starting to ravage his body. He became progressively insane and blind and at the time of his death he was confined to his private apartments, often in a straightjacket. He died in 1820 at the age of eighty-two. He and Queen Charlotte had fifteen children, and his son George IV succeeded him.

The War of 1812

There was a "Second War for Independence" as it was sometimes called when the United States, during James Madison's presidency, declared war on Great Britain in June 1812. The Royal Navy was seizing American ships when they were caught violating the British blockade to Napoleonic France. Additionally, the British captured American seamen and forced them into service in the Royal Navy. The United States cut off all trade with Europe, a tactic which was harder on the Americans than on the British. But Congress had an ulterior motive for this war. They believed it opened the way to expand the country north into Canada, which was still in the hands of the king. The war was tougher than both the Americans and British expected, and in December 1814 it ended with the Treaty of Ghent with nothing really accomplished or changed.

For the most part, the War of 1812 had little impact on Bucks County, although the citizens of the county did rally to prepare themselves in the event the enemy came too close. Once again, the taverns of Bucks County played a role in history when many of them across the county became the designated meeting places where residents gathered to form volunteer companies, drill in preparation and march when asked to protect their country. According to W.W. Davis's *History of Bucks County*, one meeting was held at Charles Hinkle's tavern in Newtown and a volunteer company was formed there. This effort was followed by residents of Bristol, Bensalem, Middletown and the Doylestown region, who also pledged themselves "to march at a moment's notice" in case the "Fourth District" was invaded.

W.W. Davis reports in his account about Bucks County's involvement in the War of 1812:

> *The quota from this county, consisting of 88 artillery and 814 infantry and riflemen, to be taken from the first and second classes of the enrolled militia, was called for the 12th of August. They were taken from the four old militia regiments, and consolidated into a battalion…assembled at Thomas Bean's Tavern, Warminster…to march to Marcus Hook.*

Bucks Countians, this time united as citizens of the United States and not divided by patriotism versus loyalty to the Crown, fought valiantly in the second and last war America fought against the British.

Chapter 4

Spas, Baths and Resorts

'Tis hard to tell which is best: Music, Food, Drink, or Rest.
—Unknown

There was an ever growing need for more taverns, inns and ferry stops after the American War for Independence. More roads were added, other roads expanded, the Delaware Canal came into existence and railroad stations popped up in almost every major town. The established public houses were expanded, often with one or two stories added above the original structure. Farmers and tradesmen, home from their commissions in the war, were back to transporting their goods and livestock to Philadelphia markets and New Jersey ports. Stagecoach routes grew to accommodate the increase in travelers who came to Bucks County either on business or to enjoy the summer "resorts" that were growing along the Delaware and inland. City dwellers longed for the clean air and cool breezes that the countryside afforded them, and many of the more wealthy Philadelphians summered in the larger inns with their families.

It is impossible to recount every tavern that was in existence in Bucks County during the eighteenth and nineteenth centuries. Many changed ownership frequently, and with the change of proprietorship the names were also changed. Often the tavern buildings were turned into private homes, markets or general stores, and too many others burned down as fire was very common in the kitchens of these establishments. Still, the number of these buildings that remain completely intact is amazing, and even more astounding is the fact that scores of them have continued to serve patrons uninterrupted throughout the past three hundred years.

Each has its own story; each has its own character and in some cases a ghost or two. Their present owners are just as eager to please their guests as the owners of the 1600s, 1700s and 1800s, and regardless of the support afforded by modern technology, they work equally as hard. Political events are still discussed within their walls, people fall in and out of love across their tables and business is still conducted on their barstools. In other words, these inns and taverns are still making history.

Lower Bucks County

The earliest taverns in Bucks County were opened at the lower end of the county following the establishment of King's Road, and even before the building of the first governor's mansion, Pennsbury Manor.

Bristol, which was called Buckingham at first and then New Bristol until it was incorporated as Bristol, is located in the southern portion of Bucks County along the Delaware, and was settled around 1681 by Samuel Clift. It was located in an area that was easily navigable by oceangoing vessels and became a busy port. Bristol experienced its earliest growth when the King's Highway was built from Philadelphia to northern parts of the county, leading directly through Bristol. It has been a vital and integral part of Bucks County ever since that time, growing steadily from a bustling port and a convenient stop along King's Highway to a resort offering what was believed to be the restorative chalybeate (Latin for "full of iron") waters of the Bath Springs, and as a residence to several of Philadelphia's most distinguished aristocrats. Bristol's visitors ranged from the very wealthy to the very poor, and it has been a thriving center of commerce and industry—a home to shipbuilders in its early years, as well as to sawmills and gristmills and eventually numerous manufactories.

It also was the first county seat of Bucks County, and most of the justice had been handed out from the taverns in Bristol until a two-story courthouse was erected in 1705, complete with gallows and whipping post. The second floor was used as a courtroom and the first floor the prison. Court was held in Bristol from 1705 until 1725 when it was moved to Newtown, which was more centrally located within the county.

Bristol was the site of two yearly fairs and markets, one in May and one in October. Those who attended these festive events could shop at the market booths, purchase livestock and dance to music played in the open. Although the Bristol residents complained about the rowdiness of the festivities, the fairs continued for more than twenty years.

Bristol's beautiful mansions attest to its notable affluence and the important role it played in the history of Bucks County. Thriving businessmen, shipbuilders, merchants, traders and diplomats made Bristol their home. As the county seat Bristol was the center of activity, and taverns and inns were built along the riverside to accommodate its many visitors coming to town for court. Records in Doylestown show that ten public houses were licensed in Bristol from the early 1700s.

These hotels accommodated the many wealthy and distinguished people who traveled near and far by boat or stagecoach to enjoy the mineral springs. Vacationers had a choice of the King George II, the General Brown, the King of Prussia, the Cross Keys, the Rising Sun, the Patton House, the Cottage House, the Farmers' Hotel, the Exchange Hotel, the Bath or the Yellow Tavern.

In the early 1800s, the notoriety of the healing effects of the mineral springs grew, especially after Dr. Benjamin Rush—who served in the Continental Congress and was a signer of the Declaration of Independence—gave a talk on the healing effects of the water. Each season hundreds of people arrived in Bristol to vacation, and Dr. Joseph

P. Minnick, who owned the grounds around the springs, built the Bath and Badger Racecourse to complete the resort environment.

It was in Bristol that sitting Vice President Aaron Burr spent the evening after his famous duel with Alexander Hamilton. When the duel was over, and he saw that he had seriously wounded Hamilton, Burr traveled from New Jersey to Bristol in haste and spent the evening at the Yellow Tavern. Hamilton's wound was mortal, and he died the next day. Burr was later indicted for murder in both New York and New Jersey, although he was never tried.

The construction of the Delaware canal and the decision to make Bristol the terminal point added even further to the economic growth of the city. Excavations began in October 1827 with a groundbreaking ceremony, complete with prayers and speeches and the playing of "Hail Columbia." After the ceremony, several hundred people celebrated at the Delaware House (King George II Inn). Thousands of tons of coal transported on the canal from the Lehigh area of Pennsylvania were consigned to Bristol for shipment in sailing vessels to the Northern states.

In the mid-1800s, the environment in Bristol began to change. The development of the Philadelphia & Reading Railroad, which built more efficient ports along the Delaware for transportation of coal, seriously injured Bristol's economy. At the same time, the Saratoga Springs in upstate New York were opened and the Baths in Bristol had lost their attraction. Many of the hotels closed and became private homes or were renovated for other uses. Although the springs were closed and the coal port and shipbuilding businesses waned, Bristol remained an industrial and commercial center, and numerous mills, including the William H. Grundy Company Mills, were built and flourished in the late nineteenth century and early twentieth century.

Bristol remained vibrant and strong throughout the years. Radcliffe and Mill Streets are still busy thoroughfares even though the city is more residential now. The Bristol Riverside Theatre provides cultural activities, and there is the Bristol Lions Park along the riverfront, with sculptures that represent the nationalities of the immigrants who lived and worked in Bristol, which is truly proud of its rich diversity. And perhaps one of the most reminiscent icons is the historic riverboat cruises that leave from the same wharf where newly built ships and steamboats once left the banks of Pennsylvania for Europe and more exotic ports.

King George II Inn

The oldest continuously operated establishment in Bucks County is located on Radcliffe Street. When he received a grant of 262 acres along the Delaware River from the provincial governor of New York in 1680—two years before William Penn received the Pennsylvania land grant from the king—Samuel Clift was instructed to establish a ferry that "connected" Bristol to Burlington, New Jersey. As was the custom at that time, he also built an inn so that passengers using the ferry would have a place to stay either while waiting to cross the river or after arrival on the Pennsylvania side. Clift called his inn the Ferry House, and it's very likely that the tavern was run by Clift's

Above and below: Today, the King George Inn II retains its historical integrity and is still one of the premier restaurants in Bristol. *Courtesy of John and Geri Caparrelli, Owners.*

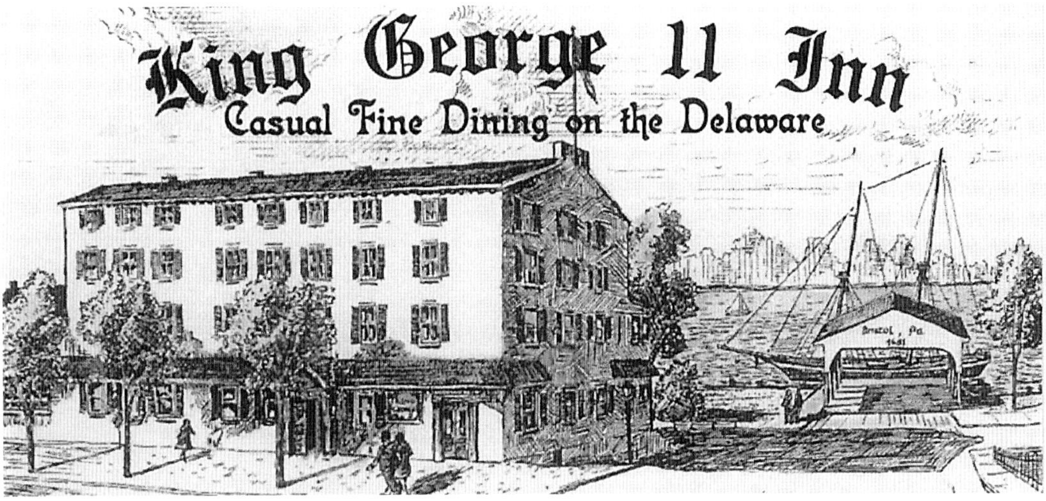

Originally called the Ferry House, the King George Inn II is the oldest continuously run establishment in Bucks County. *Courtesy of John and Geri Caparrelli, Owners.*

wife, Jane, and daughter and son-in-law, Hannah and Joseph English Jr., while Samuel ran the ferry.

The establishment has had numerous names since then, such as the Ferry Inn, King George II, King George III, the Fountain House, Ye Olde Delaware House and its present name, which is once again King George II Inn. It is said that George Washington slept there—albeit before he became the famous general and first president of the United States. It seems he stayed there on his way to Connecticut to seek a commission. The Ferry House changed hands three times between the years 1681 to 1765.

In 1765, Charles Besonett came into ownership of the inn and rebuilt it after a fire destroyed most of the original building. It was Besonett who changed the inn's name to King George III. At the outbreak of the Revolution a party of patriot troops marching through Bristol saw the sign with the name of the king they were rebelling against and opened fire on it until it was riddled with holes and destroyed. Besonett quickly renamed the tavern and inn the Fountain House.

The inn was integral during the Revolutionary War, when Washington headquartered a third of his army there under Colonel Cadwalader that infamous December 1776. Cadwalader took up residence at the inn—the sign now changed from the image of King George II to that of General Washington—and his troops were spread out in the area. It was in the Fountain House that Cadwalader waited for word from General Washington as to whether the Christmas night crossing would take place after the weather had turned stormy. When it was confirmed by note that the attack on Trenton would indeed take place, Cadwalader oversaw the crossing of his troops across the brutally cold and rushing water. The river was wider at Bristol than it was farther up at McKonkey's Ferry where Washington's troops were crossing, and although he was able to get his men across to the New Jersey side, the weather and wide rushing waters filled with ice floes prevented his artillery from crossing the river that Christmas night.

Four days later, during the second crossing of the Delaware, Cadwalader was able to succeed in getting both his men and artillery across and was integral in the success of the attack on the British in Princeton on December 29.

Besonett established the first line of stage wagons from Philadelphia to New York. With a fare of four dollars, passengers could reach New York in two days. No longer a rough ferry tavern, the inn was transformed into a refined stagecoach hotel in 1768. It was the rendezvous spot for John Adams and his wife Abigail when she traveled from Boston to Philadelphia to join him while he served his country as one of its founding fathers.

When Bristol became a popular spa resort hosting people from all parts of the East Coast, the name of the inn was changed again, this time to Ye Olde Delaware House. The guests who stayed at the Delaware House enjoyed beautiful views of the river from their rooms and often stayed for weeks at the summer retreat. One of their frequent visitors was Joseph Bonaparte, the older brother of Napoléon I, who escaped France to avoid being apprehended after his brother was arrested and sent into perpetual exile at St. Helena. He lived in New Jersey and visited Bristol often.

Throughout the years, during the world wars and Prohibition, and through the changes that took place throughout Bristol's history, the hotel and tavern remained important in Bucks County and provided a hub of social life. In the mid-1900s, the inn's name was changed back to the King George II once again. Still located at the corner of Radcliffe and Mill streets, this vibrant establishment is owned by Geri and John Caparrelli today.

The Caparrellis proudly celebrated the 325th anniversary of the King George II Inn in 2006 with a very special reception, reminiscent of the days when this old hotel was the premier social scene of Bucks County. "Someone told me that the King George II is a diamond and I agree," Geri said. "It needs rediscovering because it is so special. We know we must keep the integrity of its history." In commemoration of the anniversary, the Caparrellis had a plaque designed that lists every proprietor of the inn and the dates they owned it. They display it proudly on the door to the dining room.

Red Lion Inn (King's Road)

Although certainly the oldest and possibly the most favored, Bristol was not the only place where travelers received food and lodging in the early days of Bucks County. The King's Road played a huge role in the establishment of towns and boroughs north of Bristol, and along with settlements, licenses for taverns and inns were requested and granted.

The Red Lion Inn (not to be confused with the Red Lion Inn of Newtown) was one of the first inns to be located on the King's Road, which at the time was still just a wilderness road through unbroken forest. Although it is thought that the Red Lion had been in operation as early as 1710, the liquor license was officially granted to Philip Amos in 1730. It was a solid stone building with piazzas on two sides and set in

FERRY
SCHEDULE OF RATES
SEPTEMBER 1753

SINGLE FOOT PASSENGERS......................6 PENCE
TWO PERSONS AT THE SAME TIME..........4 PENCE
THREE OR MORE....................................3 PENCE EACH
SINGLE HORSE AND RIDER......................1 SHILLING
ANY GREATER NUMBER ....9 PENCE
SINGLE OX..1 SHILLING 3 PENCE
ANY GREATER NUMBER........................1 SHILLING
SHEEP...2 PENCE EACH
HOGS (ALIVE)...6 PENCE
(DEAD) ....3 PENCE
FOUR WHEELED CARRIAGES W/TWO HORSE AND ONE PERSON
..5 SHILLINGS
TWO WHEELED CARRIAGES WITH A SINGLE HORSE AND ONE PERSON...2 SHILING 6 PENCE

Schedule of Fares per J. H. Battle's History of Bucks County

Early fares for the ferry at Bristol that connected to Burlington, New Jersey, were recorded in J.H. Battle's *History of Bucks County Pennsylvania.*

a picturesque landscape with a winding stream and old stone bridge. When Amos died, his wife continued to run the tavern, and delegates from the first Continental Congress dined there in 1774 when meeting the Pennsylvania delegates. In 1781, a division of the Continental Army on their way to Yorktown encamped at the Red Lion Inn.

National House/Stagecoach Inn

In the peaceful little village of Fallsington a license was requested for a public house to be established in a building belonging to John Merrick, the local tanner. With the development of the King's Road, the villagers were seeing a greater number of travelers come through Fallsington and so the license was granted. Serving both stagecoach passengers and the local farmers on their way to markets in Philadelphia, the tavern became the center of activity, used as a tavern, an inn and even the local jailhouse until prisoners could be moved to Doylestown. The inn was expanded after the Civil War and the name changed to the National House. The tavern was in continuous use until it closed during Prohibition. Renamed the Stagecoach Inn, it is now an attraction on the walking tour given by Historic Fallsington, Inc.

The Stagecoach Inn is a perfect example of an early tavern that catered to the local community as well as stagecoach passengers. *Courtesy of Historic Fallsington, Inc.*

The Robert Morris and the Alexander Hotel

Morrisville, at one time considered a possible location for the capital of the United States, claimed two taverns named for Revolutionary heroes. The Robert Morris, named for the second owner of Summerseat in Morrisville and the gentleman who has been heralded as the financier of the War for Independence, and the Alexander Hotel, named for General William Alexander, known also as Lord Sterling.

Bensalem and Dunks Ferry Hotel

Many wealthy and influential Philadelphians built country estates in Bensalem in the late 1600s to escape the noise and dirt of the city where their businesses were located. Since travel along the river was the most efficient route, ferries and inns sprouted up along the banks of the Delaware to offer food and rest for those traveling on the river to their estates.

Following on King's Road and located in Bensalem Township, the Dunks Ferry was a pre-Revolutionary ferry that carried Pennsylvanians across the Delaware at a spot

Pen Ryn was one of the earliest and finest estates in Bucks County, and was the setting for a romantic elopement organized by Benjamin Franklin. It is still a romantic location for many brides and grooms each year. *Courtesy of Pen Ryn Mansion.*

now known as Cornwells Heights near Bristol. Started by Duncan Williamson, it was the site where Colonel Cadwalader was to cross the Delaware on Christmas night 1776, but was stalled because of the severe weather. As the years passed, Dunks Ferry Hotel became a place of recreation for wealthy Philadelphians who came to the area for the excellent shad fishing and duck hunting that was available in Bucks County.

Pen Ryn Mansion

Although it wasn't a tavern or inn in the early years of Bucks County, the Penn Ryn Mansion, one of the oldest estates in the Philadelphia region, was certainly a home that welcomed many travelers of importance and people of distinction through its doors. And because it serves as one of Bucks County's premier catering establishments today, it's interesting to touch upon its history and the stories that keep this 250-year-old estate alive in Bucks Countians' hearts.

The land purchased by Abraham Bickley, a wealthy shipping merchant and an alderman in the very early days of Philadelphia, was originally called Belle Voir. And although it certainly does have a beautiful view of the Delaware River, Bickley changed

The master of Pen Ryn Mansion would stick his head through this "powder room" door to have his wig powdered while keeping his clothing clean. It is still a part of the mansion today. *Courtesy of Pen Ryn Mansion.*

the name of the estate to Pen Ryn to reflect the home of his ancestry in Cornwall in Great Britain. The mansion was built in 1744 along the Delaware by Abraham's son Samuel in what is called Andalusia in Bensalem Township. In its oldest section, a generous entrance hall sat between what was originally the dining room with fine wood paneling and a parlor complete with a "powder room," where the lord of the manor could open a hole in a door and stick his head inside while servants powdered his wig without soiling his clothes. Samuel's son, Abraham III, enlarged the building when he became the proprietor to accommodate his large family and added a Palladian window, a rather new architectural design of that period.

At the time of his marriage to Mary Shewell, he had purchased a coach from London that was exactly like one owned by George Washington and used on his inauguration day. It bore the family coat of arms on the door and was drawn by four bay horses, which were perfectly matched. It was driven by a coachman who was also accompanied by two footmen that stood on the back of the coach.

None of the children of Abraham III and Mary Shewell married, and there were no heirs to inherit the beautiful Pen Ryn. Abraham IV offered to leave the estate to his cousin Lloyd Wharton, providing that Wharton hyphenate his name to Wharton-Bickley, which he reluctantly agreed to do. Upon Lloyd's death the estate was left to his son, Robert. Robert's cousin Lucy Wharton Drexel, the widow of Joseph Drexel, a member of one of Philadelphia's wealthiest banking families, purchased the estate from him. Lucy and her daughters loved the estate and added additional wings, gardens and terraces. They entertained extensively, including Lucy's niece, Mother Katharine Drexel, who was canonized a Roman Catholic saint in 2000. Lucy left the estate to her daughter Josephine Drexel Henry who was the last to use the estate as a residence, but during the many years that the house remained in the Bickley, Wharton-Bickley, Drexel and Biddle families—all related—it was the site of elegant banquets, fashionable picnics and exceptional weddings.

Between 1946 and 1988, the house served as the Pen Ryn Episcopal School. Then the property, which was going to be developed, sat vacant and dormant when plans to establish a housing development on the estate fell through. This once prosperous and beloved home of some of the wealthiest families in the Philadelphia region was vandalized and left to ruin for five years. Its radiators leaked until walls started to crumble, and the once beautiful gardens became overgrown and filled with weeds.

The mansion was offered at auction several times during this period but not sold until coinvestors William Haas, Gerald Donohue and Anthony Szuszczewicz made an offer to purchase the neglected estate and restore the mansion to its original dignity and splendor. It took two years to renovate the house, but it was a productive two years. Some of the important architectural details that had been removed when the house became a school were found in the carriage house or returned by local residents who had taken them for safekeeping. Even the "wig door" was found along with pieces of the rose marble fireplaces. As luck would have it, the original coach that was purchased by Abraham III was found and returned to its home in Andalusia. When Haas and his coinvestors purchased the nine-acre estate, they partnered with the Bucks County Department of Parks,

The Bickley carriage was identical to the one used by George Washington on his inauguration day. It recently was returned to Pen Ryn Mansion after it was mistakenly believed to be President Washington's. *Courtesy of Pen Ryn Mansion.*

which purchased the surrounding eighty acres to ensure that the property would remain undeveloped.

They have also restored the carriage house and named it Belle Voir to reflect the original name of the land. It is used to cater larger events. Pen Ryn is a favorite site of brides who desire the romance and elegance of this beautiful location along the Delaware as the background for their weddings, and rightfully so since its history is filled with stories of love and romance—both tragic and happy.

In fact, Pen Ryn was the setting of one of the most romantic stories told in Bucks County, and the cast of characters—in addition to the main protagonists who were artist Benjamin West and Philadelphia socialite Elizabeth Shewell—include Francis Hopkinson, William White and the legendary Benjamin Franklin.

Benjamin West, the artist mentioned earlier in this book who painted tavern signs during his "starving artist" years, and Elizabeth Shewell had fallen in love before he left for London to establish himself as a portraitist. They became engaged to be married, but Elizabeth's brother, Stephen Shewell, a merchant and shipping tycoon, was thoroughly against the idea of his sister marrying a lowly artist, no matter how talented he may be. Stephen, who had been Elizabeth's guardian since the death of their parents, locked Elizabeth in her room under guard until the ship Benjamin West was taking to London set sail, preventing any chance of her leaving with her betrothed.

The artist quickly established himself and fell in favor with King George III. He painted several members of the royal family to great acclaim. Now that his reputation and purse were growing steadily, he sent for Elizabeth, asking his father to escort her

Benjamin West's portrait of his wife and son. (See endnote 21.) *Courtesy of the Cleveland Museum of Art.*

to London personally. When Stephen got word of the plans, he sent Elizabeth to her sister, Mary Shewell Bickley, at Pen Ryn with strict instructions to keep her locked in one of the rooms upstairs.

It was known throughout Philadelphia that the domineering Stephen had promised Elizabeth to another man despite her objections. Hopkinson, White and Franklin must have either felt great pity for the girl or were romantics at heart for they persuaded the sea captain of a ship bound for London to hold off sailing until a "certain lady" was brought onboard. Then they brought a knotted rope to Pen Ryn, gave it to a serving girl who concealed it under her skirt and instructed her to bring it up to Elizabeth's room. With the help of the rope, a cedar tree outside the second-story window and Benjamin West's father in a rowboat that was tied out of sight on the Delaware, the three gentlemen helped Elizabeth flee from her brother's tyranny.

Benjamin West was waiting for her at the dock in London and they were married immediately. They never returned to America, although Elizabeth did try to reach out to her brother several times to no avail. Her husband painted a beautiful portrait of Elizabeth and their infant son, which hangs in the Cleveland Museum of Art.[21]

Francis Hopkinson was a young Philadelphia lawyer at the time and later became a member of the Continental Congress and a signer of the Declaration of Independence. Benjamin Franklin—inventor, statesman, printer—was a frequent visitor to Pen Ryn. William Whyte, who was only eighteen years old at the time, later became the first bishop of Pennsylvania.

It may also be interesting to note that just three years later, in 1767, Benjamin Franklin was in a very similar situation to Stephen Shewell in that his own daughter, Sarah "Sally" Franklin, insisted upon a marriage that her father was very much against. Franklin's wife Deborah, however, intervened and allowed Sally to wed Richard Bache despite her husband's protests. We have to wonder if Benjamin Franklin was thinking something similar to: "What goes around comes around."

Chapter 5

Where the Court Meets, the Lanes End and Points Between and Beyond

May you never forget what is worth remembering or remember what is best forgotten.
—An Irish toast

As the roads were expanded north and inland from the Delaware River, more settlements grew. Many of these villages, boroughs and townships played a role in the American Revolution, the Underground Railroad and the growth of trade and travel to and from Philadelphia and New York. In many cases, many of these towns are as quaint and charming today as they were more than two hundred years ago, although their roads are more crowded and their meadows and pastures have been taken over by expensive housing developments.

Despite—or perhaps because of—the development and growth they have experienced, especially over the past twenty years, their residents maintain their history and architectural integrity. The sons and daughters of these places are generous in sharing their ancestral "homes," and the towns and boroughs are living museums that do more than hint of the past—they bring you back to the simple, wholesome living that their founders practiced, all while providing what their present residents need for living in a contemporary world.

Keeping this delicate balance is not always easy, but it is always rewarding. It's inspiring to meet volunteers who spend uncountable hours each year working at their local historical associations and societies, documenting photos and personal journals, collecting and preserving artifacts and helping researchers and genealogists record history. It is heartwarming to meet couples who have purchased historical landmarks and, despite the work and cost involved, are committed to preserving the character and integrity of the buildings by spending hours researching and working closely with architects and historic paint analysts. It is amazing to find present innkeepers spending hundreds of thousands of dollars in renovation and upkeep to make certain that their establishments are as inviting and charming as they were hundreds of years before their ownership.

They all appreciate that homes built over the centuries *should* be saved and protected. They understand the great architectural significance they have as portals to reach back into the periods of history that shaped who we are as a nation.

Newtown

When William Penn was riding in the countryside with friends, he remarked to the party he was with, "This is the place proposed for my new town."[22] And so it was called Newtown or New Township on several maps. William Penn believed in the careful design and layout of towns and cities and hired Thomas Holme as the first surveyor general of Pennsylvania to plan the city of Philadelphia. Then, when accompanying his surveyor north of the city in what was to become Bucks County, Penn claimed seven thousand acres that he called his "New Township." In 1692 there was at least one man living in Newtown named Cornelius Spring, although there may have been several more residents.

When Penn sold land to purchasers, it was with the proviso that they would form a township center when the land ownership reached five to ten thousand acres in total. This was fully carried out in Newtown. Sixteen wedge-shaped farms were laid out, varying in acreage, with the town common at the center, "…for the convenience of roads, passage to ye water, and other benefits to ye said township."[23] Forty acres had been preserved on either side of the Newtown creek for this purpose.

Newtown is one of the oldest towns in the county, and next to Bristol it was probably one of the most important. Durham Road was the first of the byways to reach Newtown, and ten more roads from neighboring townships followed the boundaries of the tracks of land owned by the local farmers. By 1726, the county seat was moved from Bristol to Newtown, and out of necessity Newtown changed from a farming community to a bustling, crowded center of government.

Before the Revolution there were five inns all located within easy walking distance of one another. There was also a jailhouse, a courthouse, numerous businesses and private homes. As the county seat, Newtown was the polling place of both lower and middle Bucks County every October 2. On that day, the town came alive with horse races and booths lined up along the streets laden with pies, cakes and beer.

The Newtown Library was established as early as 1760, and the Newtown Academy, a school for higher education, was built for $4,000. The school's charter called for ten poor children to be educated gratis in addition to its paying students. Many of its graduates went on to pursue a university education, followed by careers in law, medicine and teaching.

General George Washington had set up his headquarters at Summerseat in Morrisville when he first arrived in Pennsylvania after being chased across New Jersey by the British, but at some point before December 24, 1776, he designated a private home in Newtown as his "quarters." He sent his secretary with all his papers for safekeeping to the house of John Harris and after the Battle of Trenton, made that house his headquarters. While in Newtown, he entertained Hessian officers who were his prisoners, and met with his own officers to orchestrate plans for another daring attack against the British in Princeton. As the war progressed, Newtown continued to play an integral role in the Revolution for at least two years until the battles moved to the Southern colonies.

On December 26, 1776, General Washington made the house of John Harris his headquarters in Newtown. The house burned down and was rebuilt on the same site but unfortunately was razed in the 1900s. *Courtesy of the Newtown Historical Association.*

Newtown continued to be the county seat until 1813 when the center of government for Bucks County moved to Doylestown. Yet Newtown remained a busy cultural and commercial hub even as the crowds traveled northward to Doylestown.

Many of the original structures in Newtown—from the early brick and stone town homes to the beautiful Georgian and Victorian mansions—are beautifully maintained and carefully restored. Even the sidewalks retain the feel of Colonial America.

The Sign of the Bird in Hand

> *To his Majesty's Justices of the Peace for the Court of Quarter Sessions Held at Bristoll this day the 13th of June 1723:*
>
> *The Humble Petition of Agnis Welsh Shewing her deplorable Condition her husband being a prisoner and having a great family of Children that is Maintain'd by her keeping a house of Entertainment therefore Pray the Honourable Justices to grant her a Recommendation for the Ensueing Year, that she may be in a Capacity to maintain her Children and your Petitioner as in Duty Bound shall Ever pray & c.*
>
> *The Mark of Agnis X Welch*[24]

George and Agnes Welsh established the "Old Frame Tavern" where the "Red Lyon Inn" had been located since about 1686. It was later called "Bird in Hand" by owner Tamar Carey. *Courtesy of the Newtown Historical Association.*

To the Court of Quarter Sessions to be held at Newtown for the County of Bucks the 15th Day of June 1727

To the Honourable Bench of His Majesties Jusitices of the peace Greeting.

Humble Sheweth

Whereas Your Petitioner hath heretofore kept a Public House of entertainment for the accommodation of People at Court times and travelers, and in as much as Your Petitioner hath been recommended by You heretofore to the Governor for his License, therefore these are to Request that you would be pleased to grant the like favor for which Your Humble Petitioner shall as in Duty bound ever pray & c.

George Welsh[25]

To the Justices of the peace Now Sitting at Newtowne

The Humble Petition of Agnes Welsh a poor widow

Sheweth that She being a widow and a family of Small Children without any help to maintaine but her Small Endeavors in selling Cakes and Some Liquor at publick times That the Grand jury are pleased to take Notice thereof in order to prevent your pett'r from takeing the Said means towards the Mantainance of her said Small family without which your Pet'r will be rend'red uncapable of Supporting them & for as much as your Pett'r only Desires to follow the same at publick times.

The Newtown Reliance Company for the Detection and Apprehension of Horse Thieves was founded at the Bird in Hand in 1819. *Courtesy of the Newtown Historical Association.*

> *May it therefore please the worshipfull Bench to Consider the Premises and the nature of your Pett'r's Circumstances and grant your Pett'r Liberty to use her poor endeavors for maintaining her family as affore s'd*
> *And She will pray & c. (unsigned)*[26]

From what we read in the first petition of Agnes Welsh, life must not have been easy for her—a husband in jail and a large family to care for. Yet she was industrious enough to take on the monumental business of running a public house to support her family until her husband was released from incarceration for an unknown crime. She received her first license in 1723 for a public house, assumed to be on the site of a previous tavern called the Red Lyon Inn owned by the Walley family, one of Newtown's original settler families. The building was built ca.1680 and was located on State Street (a stretch of Durham Road). The Welshes called it the Old Frame Tavern.

George Welsh added onto the frame building, and it now had projecting eaves and a hipped roof that sloped at the back. It was the largest tavern in the town and it measured sixty feet long and thirty feet wide. Inside, the barkeeper would serve beverages through a small opening from behind a cage-like bar.

Ownership of the tavern passed from the Welsh family to several other owners, although it isn't clear who owned the tavern during the Revolution. We do know that the Bird in Hand was the site of the only important skirmish fought in Newtown. In February 1778 the British were in control of Philadelphia and Newtown was being guarded by the colonial militia. Tailors were in the Bird In Hand sewing uniforms for

Hessian prisoners were held in the Bird in Hand, the Brick Hotel, the Presbyterian Church and the jail. An original cell door is located in the Bird in Hand. This also was the site of the only skirmish fought in Newtown during the Revolution. *Courtesy of Jonathan and Elizabeth Hunt.*

soldiers of the Continental Army, now located at Valley Forge. A young soldier, who had been ill and needed to remain behind when his own regiment left Newtown, was told to guard the tavern.

Armed loyalists raided the town. From his garret window, the boy shot several of the enemy, holding them off for as long as he could before he himself was mortally wounded. The Tories invaded the Bird In Hand and confiscated two thousand yards of material. According to J.H. Battle's *History of Bucks County*, the boy was buried in a vacant lot at the upper end of town, but there is no tombstone that marks the grave so its exact location is not known. He was not the only soldier to lose his life that day. Five American soldiers were killed, four wounded and eleven captured.

In the years following the war, Asa Carey, a widower who didn't have much money, was the last person to hold the position of jailer when it was in Newtown, and when the county seat moved to Doylestown, he went with it to keep his job. Before long, he decided he wasn't happy there, resigned and returned to Newtown.

At that time Tamar Worstall was doing a good business selling her baked goods from a two-story stone house. She was financially comfortable, renowned for her ginger cakes and pies, and she was an old maid. Asa asked her to marry him and she agreed. The following year, in 1817, Tamar sold her interest in the bakery and bought the Old Frame House. Edward Hicks painted a sign for Tamar replicating the proverb, "A bird in the hand is worth two in the bush."[27] There, she and Asa lived out the rest of their lives as the Bird In Hand's tavern keepers. Tamar kept the tavern impeccable and provided meals and her notoriously delicious ginger cakes, bread, biscuits and pies, while Asa tended bar. It was the gathering place for important meetings, politicians and associations. One of them was the Newtown Reliance Company, one of Newtown's oldest organizations offering insurance against horse theft, which was founded at the Bird in Hand.

After the death of the postmaster, Asa was appointed to the job and he kept the mail and papers locked in a cupboard behind the bar where he also kept his liquor. Asa was also appointed librarian of Newtown Library Company, and the books and papers were moved to the Bird In Hand. His annual salary was one dollar and the privilege of reading the books for free.

When Asa died at the age of eighty-five, Tamar continued to run the tavern until three years before her death in 1842. She was eighty years old when she died. They had at least one daughter, Sarah, who was courted by and married William B. Coale, the editor of the *Bucks County Bee* newspaper.

The Bird In Hand, whether run as a tavern, a quaint shop or owned as a private residence, has retained its name and its sign over the last 250 years. It is a Newtown landmark, along with its beautiful perennial gardens and outbuildings. Today the Bird In Hand is a private home owned by Jonathan and Elizabeth Hunt.

Brick Hotel

Shadrach Walley was one of the original owners of land in Penn's "New Township." His title passed to his only son John, then to John's son Joseph. There is confusion as

The old frame house has changed very little over the years, and the privately owned home is still a well-known and beloved landmark in Newtown. *Courtesy of Jonathan and Elizabeth Hunt.*

to where their tavern, called the Red Lion, was built and operated on the Walley land. When Amos Strickland Sr. purchased the Walley interests in 1750 in a sheriff's sale, the records show that a hotel and a half acre of ground adjoining it were excluded from the bill of sale. This is the property that bordered State Street and "Strickland Lane," which was later called Washington Avenue. Yet other records show that it was located where George and Agnes Welsh opened their Old Frame Tavern on State Street south of where Strickland obtained his land. It is entirely possible that since records of licenses were not always kept carefully in the very early years, or were burned in house fires, both corners in Newtown could have had taverns called Red Lion—or Lyon—at some point in the seventeenth or early eighteenth centuries.

When Joseph Walley died in 1760, one tavern was being managed by George Dunn, and the property was sold—again at a sheriff's sale and again to Amos Strickland—who by now was county commissioner and a Quaker minister in addition to being a Newtown farmer.

In 1763, Strickland began construction of a two-story brick building, which was beautifully detailed inside and out. The ornate paneling and artistry of the woodworking in the house is said to have equaled the elegance and workmanship in the finest houses in Philadelphia. This is where Strickland lived with his second wife and four children: Amos Jr., Rachel, Elizabeth and Frances.

The Brick Hotel has held a prominent place in Bucks County history since the eighteenth century. *Courtesy of the Newtown Historical Association.*

The Brick Hotel held a prominent place in the events of the Revolution in December 1776. It was for a time General Greene's headquarters before the crossing that led to the Battle of Trenton, and Generals Washington, Greene and Sterling, among others, met there several times while planning their surprise attacks in Princeton. On December 27, 1776, the Hessian officers who survived the battle of Trenton and were captured were brought to the Brick Hotel. General Washington gave strict orders that they were to be treated with respect, and General Alexander hosted a dinner for them in the dining room.

Strickland died in 1779 and left the property to his son Amos, who sold the hotel to his sister Rachel and her husband Mark Hapenny. The Brick Hotel was eventually sold to Charles Hinkle, who named it the Coach and Horse. When Bucks Countians heard of the burning of Washington during the War of 1812, men gathered at Hinkle's tavern to organize a volunteer company and raise troops—the first in the county to offer services to the president.

But perhaps the most famous of all the owners of the Brick Hotel was Major Joseph O. Archambault. Archambault was born in France in 1798. At the age of ten, when he became an orphan, he entered the Emperor Bonaparte's Riding School at St. Cloude where he was educated in literacy as well as trained in military horsemanship. After attending the school for six years he joined the emperor's army, but a year later the emperor was taken prisoner and sent to St. Helena. Because of his loyalty to the emperor and his excellent skill with horses, Archambault was chosen as one of eighteen people to accompany the emperor in his perpetual exile to oversee the care

Known for its intricate interior moldings, the Brick's character remains intact today and is still a favored hotel of visitors to Newtown. *Courtesy of the Newtown Historical Association.*

of Napoléon's horses, and through that assignment he became a close friend of the emperor, who was known for his camaraderie with his soldiers. A little over a year later, the English decided that it was too expensive to support Bonaparte's large entourage and Archambault was sent first to the Cape of Good Hope and then to England.

He couldn't bear to live in Europe without Napoléon, and he emigrated from France to New York where he lived for three years, married and taught French to the son of a fellow passenger on the ship he took to America. He moved to Philadelphia and frequently visited Joseph Bonaparte, the emperor's brother, and undoubtedly vacationed in Bristol at the spas with him. He came to Newtown in 1821, and took over the management of the Brick Hotel from Charles Hinkle in 1825.

He bought the property in 1829, and added a third story to the main building and a wide porch on the front and side. The first floor had a barroom, a dining room and three parlors. It included stables, an icehouse and additional outbuildings that proved convenient for many of his guests. The Brick was considered a first-class hotel, and during the years that wealthy tourists came to Bucks County to enjoy the baths and springs at Bristol, the Brick Hotel became a summer destination and resort since it was convenient to Bristol via Durham Road (State Street in Newtown).

During the 1830s, Archambault became an admirer of an itinerant and eloquent minister, Frederick Plummer. Plummer had a large following, called "Plummerites," and in pleasant weather his meetings were held in the woods and in groves. One of Plummer's preaching centers was Newtown, and Archambault invited Plummer to hold his meetings at the Brick Hotel but it wasn't large enough to house all of his followers. Plummer stood in the door and preached to the large crowds standing in the street. Archambault, realizing that this was not an ideal situation, suggested to the town that a free church be built, which would be open to all ministers who came to Newtown to preach without pay. The proposal was endorsed, Archambault donated the lot and the Newtown Hall was built and opened for worship in 1831.

In the deed for the lot for this free church, Archambault stipulated that the contributions were to be used strictly for the building fund, and that if the house was not opened to all ministers who wanted to preach for free and if contributions were collected to pay a minister preaching there, the property would immediately revert back to his heirs.

When Mr. Plummer died, the enthusiasm among this sect declined and before long the free church wasn't being used at all. Archambault agreed to transfer the property to the borough.

Archambault also served as a captain and a major in the Civil War, commanding a Union troop for several years. He died in Philadelphia in 1874 at the age of seventy-eight.

The almost 250-year-old Brick Hotel was renovated in the late twentieth century and returned to its original elegance. All of the guest rooms have been restored and decorated with antiques and period furniture, and the extensive wraparound enclosed porch offers additional dining areas. It is still one of the most popular establishments in Bucks County and a favored bed-and-breakfast for tourists and businesspersons alike.

Temperance House

When the international effort to diminish or eliminate the consumption of intoxicating liquors moved through Europe and found its way to America in the 1800s, it was hugely embraced, primarily by the women who were the victims of the domestic abuse, destitution and crime affiliated with drunkenness. Societal problems, crime, ill health and every sort of misery were blamed on alcohol—usually from the pulpit. A period of humanitarian reform swept the country, and as well-organized temperance associations formed in areas like New York and Massachusetts, chapters sprouted up across the country. The movement lost steam during the Civil War but was quickly revitalized after the war, and although it didn't eliminate the use of alcohol, it certainly did curtail it.

A series of temperance meetings were held in Newtown in 1877 in Newtown Hall every evening for two weeks. The ministers from the Methodist, Episcopal and Presbyterian churches took part and brought members of their congregations who were willing to bear witness to the evils of alcohol and the benefits of being reformed. Not surprising the Society of Friends also took a leading role in the meetings. There were old, middle aged, young adults and children at these meetings, which were called "Murphy Meetings" after Francis Murphy, an Irish-born American who was the first to give testimony to the evils of being intoxicated and who was responsible for getting more than ten million signatures on temperance pledges.

Those who attended the meetings heard testimony from reformed alcoholics, who gave detailed descriptions of what life was like at their "lowest level of degradation," and the meetings became the premier form of entertainment in an age when there was not much else to do in the evening. Human drama is a big draw—whether portrayed in a play, in person by articulate speakers or as in modern times in television and movies—and this was no different in the nineteenth century. Women and children hurried to the hall early to be certain to get a good seat and stayed for the entire meeting, which adjourned at ten o'clock or later each night.

During the October 1877 temperance meetings in Newtown, seven hundred persons signed the pledge, which read:

> *National Christian Temperance Union*
> *With Malice towards None, and Charity for All.*
> *I, the undersigned do pledge my word and honor God helping me, to abstain from all intoxicating liquors as a beverage, and that I will encourage all others to abstain.*[28]

By signing the pledge, the person was promising to abstain from all intoxicating liquors, including wine, beer and cider, as well as the use of profanity. The tidal wave of good temperance in Newtown resulted in the organization of the "Newtown Branch of the National Christian Temperance Union," which met once a week to keep the momentum of temperance going. It was believed that as the temperance movement grew, taverns would drop out of existence as there would be no customers. Smart tavern owners, who realized that the movement was going to hurt their business, made changes that would keep them going—at least until the movement died down, which they expected would happen eventually.

When Andrew McGinn, the local schoolmaster, purchased a lot from Amos and Margaret Strickland in 1772 for ten pounds, temperance was furthest from his mind. He built a schoolhouse—with a tavern attached. He was married to a woman named Nancy, and according to Edward Barnsley in his book *Historic Newtown*, temperance advocate Josiah Smith said of them, "Andy and Nancy were both fond of whiskey. Nancy was the bartender in their little tavern, and with Andy, made two good customers."[29]

They sold the schoolhouse and tavern to General Francis Murray, who had been Andy's commander during the Revolutionary War. Murray had made the tavern his quarters during the winter that the Continental Army was encamped in Bucks County. After Murray's death, it was passed among several more owners, including Jolly and Mercy Yardley Longshore. Then stagecoach driver, borough constable and auctioneer Chileon W. Higgs purchased the tavern.

In response to the power of the Temperance Society, Higgs changed the name of the hotel to the Sign of the Good Samaritan and served only mineral water, mead, ginger pop and lemonade. The following article was published in the June 6, 1843 edition of the *Newtown Journal and Workingmen's Advocate*:

> *Temperance Celebration*
> *In order to celebrate and accelerate the glorious progress of the temperance cause, the friends of temperance, and the Community at large, are respectfully invited to meet at the Temperance Inn, of Chileon Higgs, in Newtown, Bucks County, on Saturday, the 17th day of June, when a sign emblematic of the principles, and most prominent features of the great reformation, will be raised…The establishment which our friend Higgs has converted into a temperance house, has been devoted for more than a century to the sale of rum. For three generations the citizens of Newtown have been exposed to its poisonous exhalations. The misery and ruin wrought, no tongue can tell, no pencil paint. After having flourished amid the sighs, and tears, and groans of more than three successive ages, it has now, at last become a monument of the irresistible progress of the temperance reformation.*

Higgs also offered an "Accommodation Line for Philadelphia via Bristol." A carriage would leave the Temperance Inn at five o'clock in the morning, travel through Attleboro (Langhorne), Hulmeville and Newportville in time to arrive in Bristol for the steamboat *Trenton*. The steamboat would then turn around and leave at two o'clock in the afternoon for Bristol, where passengers could board the carriage for the trip back to Newtown, which would arrive at six o'clock in the afternoon. The fare was sixty-two and a half cents.

William Hallowell purchased the tavern and again changed the name to the Temperance Hotel in 1848 and started serving ice cream. Then in 1865, Edward Hicks painted a sign for the next owner, Joseph Willard, that depicted a moose standing by Niagara Falls, and the name changed to the Niagara Temperance House. And when

First to abide by the Temperance movement in Newtown, Chileon Higgs's establishment became the Sign of the Good Samaritan and later changed to the Temperance House. *Courtesy of the Newtown Historical Association.*

Joseph sold the business to his brother Sam, the name was changed once again to the Temperance Hotel Oyster and Ice Cream Bar, but the locals continued to call it the Temperance House.

Today, owned by the Deon Family, the "Temp" as it is fondly referred to, is no longer dry. On the contrary, it is one of the most popular spots in Bucks County not only for the spirited fun in the tavern, but for the excellent food served in the restaurant.

Township House (The Saloon)

One of the "youngest" establishments in Newtown, the Township House, was built in 1821 on what had been part of Newtown Common, the land set aside for public use when Newtown was first surveyed by William Penn. The first tavern license requested for this site was in 1840, but when thirty-four neighbors protested that a tavern would be a "source of injury and immorality to the neighborhood," and would result in the innkeeper benefiting while "those around are reaping misery and poverty," the license was denied.[30]

However, the place must have received a license after that because during the 1880s, when the temperance movement was extremely active in Newtown, William Welsh, the proprietor at the time, had his license revoked for selling liquor to minors. Twelve witnesses from the age of fourteen to twenty testified against him. Welsh's defense was that if the witnesses were old enough to shave, they were old enough to drink. In many of the testimonies, the words, "I shave," are noted.

> *Charles Cornell testified that "I got ginger brandy: Welsh furnished it; I paid for it." On cross examination he said, "I work in the agricultural works; I get my own wages. I shave."*[31]

It didn't matter, Welsh lost his license anyway.

The frame and stone building has served many purposes over the years—it was a residence, a tavern, a school when the local schoolhouse burned down, a general store and a lawn equipment store. It was where the Catholic Mass was said during the years of 1864 to 1866 while the first Catholic Church, the Church of St. Andrew, was being built.

It was also the location of the one and only "battle" in Bucks County during the Civil War.

The American Civil War was fought for two reasons: to prevent secession of the Southern states and to end slavery. The impression we have today is that there were clear-cut opinions about slavery that met at the Mason-Dixon Line—with the North completely against slavery and the South all for it. It was never quite that clear or cut between the North and South.

Slavery had been slowly eased out in Northern states after the Revolution, but it had never been as extensively used for agriculture purposes as it had been in the Southern states. In Pennsylvania, the ownership of slaves had been eliminated with the Act for Gradual Abolition of Slavery, promoted by the Society of Friends, but the act didn't completely make black Americans "equal" with white Americans. And the word "gradual" was important in that no slave owner in Pennsylvania needed to release their slaves immediately, but only after their "investment" was paid for over a certain number of years. Many slaves remained on their former holders' estates.

Nevertheless, the call for abolition was as loud in Pennsylvania as it was in other parts of the North, but the idea was not shared by all. There was a faction of Democrats in the North who strongly opposed the Civil War. Called copperheads because of the copper liberty head coins they wore as badges, they were very vocal in their demand for peace with the Confederates. They were usually strong opponents of President Abraham Lincoln's policies, and they espoused their belief that white men should not be expected to shed blood over black slaves. Although they threatened violent resistance to the Union and the war, they never managed to become organized enough to fulfill that threat. Because they were considered treacherous and disloyal, President Lincoln had many copperhead leaders arrested and kept in prison without benefit of trial.

During the summer of the last year of the war, a party of Union soldiers on furlough was marching through Newtown from the Pennsylvania Railroad station at Croydon on their way to their homes in the northern parts of Bucks County. They were welcomed at most of the hotels and taverns along the way, treated like heroes and given free hospitality. That wasn't the case when they stopped at the Township House in Newtown, which happened to be the headquarters of the copperheads in Newtown.

The Union soldiers were refused service at the Township House by the proprietor. The barroom patrons insulted the soldiers and jeered at them, but the soldiers kept their tempers and quietly left the building to rest at the side of the road in front of the tavern. Feeling triumphant at what they considered a retreat by the soldiers, the copperheads stood at the doors and windows and continued to hurl names and insults at the soldiers. It wasn't until they called Abraham Lincoln a foul name that the unusually quiet soldiers took action.

By now patriotic citizens of Newtown had gathered nearby and were encouraging the soldiers to "do something." A man named John Buckman stood on the banks of his family's land, which was across the road from the hotel, and shouted to the soldiers to "clean out that nest of secession."[32] The soldiers did just that. They rushed back into the bar and threw out not just the copperheads, but the proprietor too. They helped themselves to refreshments, then left the borough of Newtown, walking up Durham Road to their homes in Upper Bucks County.

There was no legal action taken against the soldiers or the copperheads, but Southern sympathizers in town had John Buckman arrested for inciting a riot. The case was brought to trial in the Bucks County courts, but the jury was divided along party lines. In the meantime the war ended, and in the interest of peace the case was dropped.

The Township House became a regular gathering spot for locals in the twentieth century, and was a speakeasy in the 1940s. The tavern room houses an elaborately carved mahogany bar that was built in 1890 by the Brunswick Company, which is famous for their billiard tables and equipment, and an antique carriage has sat for many years on the front porch of the building. The Valenti family purchased the building in 1973 and decorated the restaurant with period antiques and original stained-glass windows depicting Bucks County farmlands. They sold the Township House in 2006 when they retired and the restaurant is now called The Saloon.

Justices' House

After the battles of Trenton and Princeton at the end of 1776, Brigadier General William Alexander (also known as Lord Sterling) suffered from rheumatism and gout. He was one of General Washington's most trusted officers, and had been touted by both the Americans and British for his bravery after he fought valiantly against the British in the Battle of Long Island. He was captured during that battle and subsequently released in a prisoner exchange. He was a devoted patriot, and only his health kept him temporarily from his duties in the Continental Army. It was during one of these bouts of ill health that he found himself quartered at the Justices' House in the winter of 1778.

That winter a Quaker named Thomas Watson of Buckingham hid a stack of hay from a detachment of troops who were taking whatever they could from the local farmers. His intent was to share the stack of hay with his less fortunate neighbors during the harsh winter months. However, according to Davis's *History of Bucks County*, the "landlord at Centreville" wanted to buy the stack with Continental money, which was worthless. Mr. Watson refused. He offered the landlord a fair share of the hay for free when the time came to open the stack. Disgruntled by this offer, the landlord reported Thomas Watson to the authorities, charging him with being disloyal and unwilling to accept Continental money. Watson was arrested, tried by court martial and sentenced to be hanged. All efforts by his counsel and fellow Quakers fell on deaf ears. He was confined to the Newtown jail to await his execution.

Lord Sterling was in command of Newtown that winter. According to Davis's *History of Bucks County*, after being given an exceptional meal accompanied by extra "good cheer" by his landlady, Mrs. Siddons—no doubt on purpose—the wife of Thomas Watson appeared before Lord Sterling and appealed to him for mercy on behalf of her husband.

> *He withstood her eloquence as long as he could, when he raised her to her feet and said, "Madam, you have conquered, I must relent at the tears and supplication of so noble and so good a woman as you. Your husband is saved."*

The Justices' House is a brownstone building with a frame kitchen that was built by Thomas Mayer in 1764 and adjoined an older frame structure located next door on State Street. It was purchased by George Dunn who operated a tavern in it. Then Anthony and Deborah Siddons, Benjamin Franklin's next-door neighbors in Philadelphia, purchased the property and sold their home in Philadelphia to Franklin.

It was a favorite of the justices who came to Newtown when court was in session. They gathered to talk about politics, catch up on news and exchange information. Notorious loyalist Joseph Galloway, who joined the British after the start of the Revolution, stayed at the Siddon's place so often that one of the rooms on the second floor was called the "Galloway" room. And as mentioned, it became Lord Sterling's headquarters more than once during the war.

When discussion about moving the county seat from Newtown to Doylestown started, property values dropped considerably in Newtown. The townspeople knew that before long, there wouldn't be as great a need for taverns and inns to hold the mass of people who came from all over Bucks County for court.

The Justices' House, which had been purchased in 1812 for $1,250 sold for only $812 after the county seat moved. In 1800 the Justices' House became a private residence and remains so today.

When the Justices' House came on the real estate market in 2002, thirty-year-old Geno Peruzzi purchased the house. A student of American History, with special interests in the stories of the forefathers of this country and the Revolutionary War, Geno felt compelled to purchase the historical building. He loved its simplicity, its lines,

The Justices' House was once the lodging of choice for court leaders staying in Newtown when it was the county seat. It was also the headquarters of General William Alexander (Lord Sterling) during the Revolution. *Courtesy of Geno Peruzzi.*

the original pumpkin pine floors and the fact that the huge door and original lock from the Newtown jailhouse is on the lower level of the house. His curiosity about his new home led him to the Newtown Historical Society and to the Bucks County Historical Association in Doylestown to research more about the Justices' House he had just purchased. After work in the evenings and on weekends, he poured over old deeds and ancient documents, and by the end of his first year in the house, Geno was in love—with the house and with a woman named Amy, who as it turns out, has come to love the Justices' House as much as Geno does.

The couple has hired an architect and paint analyst recommended by the Historical Architectural Review Board to help design an addition that will retain the house's historic integrity. The blueprints are finished, and the paint colors that were on the walls of the house when it was first built have been determined through paint analysis, and Geno and Amy intend to use those colors in the renovations. Their passion for safeguarding the historical character of the house is inspiring.

By coincidence, about four years after purchasing the Justices' House, Geno's uncle, who is conducting a genealogy search, found a very interesting fact that astounded the family, especially Geno. It turns out that Geno's great-great-great-great-great-

great-grandfather was one of the Hessian soldiers taken prisoner during the Battle of Trenton, a fact that no one in the family had known before. The young Hessian had been wounded in Trenton and remained in Newtown with other wounded prisoners, under the command of General Alexander who was staying at the Justices' House. After being released, the young Hessian chose to stay in the newly formed United States, and eventually he settled in Richmond Township in Berks County. His six-times-great-grandson now lives in the house where his warden had stayed during his incarceration as a prisoner of war.

Half Moon Inn (Court Inn)

In addition to the taverns and inns mentioned above, Newtown was also the home of the Half Moon Inn (also known as the Court Inn). Joseph Thornton built the oldest section of the Half Moon Inn in 1733, and ran a tavern there until his death in 1754. It was a popular gathering spot for people attending court during the time that Newtown was the county seat. Thornton's widow, Margaret, who continued to provide food and shelter for travelers to Newtown after the death of her husband, extended the building with an addition built with the extra bricks made by Amos Strickland when he built the Brick Hotel. One of the rooms, known as the Grand Jury Room, was used as a ballroom where many social events took place. At some point the name of the building was changed to the Court Inn.

Over the years it was turned into a private home, used as a schoolroom, a store and was the location of the local telephone company, which subdivided it into two units. In 1964 one part of the building was gifted to the Newtown Historical Society by Robert L. and Ruth LaRue. In 1974, the Newtown Historical Society purchased the other unit and renovated the building to its original design. It is on the National Register of Historic Places. Today it serves as a museum and historical research center, and in 2006 the building was renamed to its original Half Moon Inn. The new sign, designed by Newtown artist Rosemary Tottoroto, is a replica of the original.

Whitehall Hotel

The Whitehall Hotel was one of the premier hostelries of the county during the Victorian era. Isaac Hicks (father of the painter Edward) purchased the lot with a frame house in early 1796 and lived there until his death in 1836. During the Revolutionary War, the buildings on the lot were occupied by the quartermaster department to store military supplies. One night it was raided by the Loyalist Doan brothers, the guard was shot and the supplies were stolen.

When Isaac Hicks died, his grandson, Dr. Edward H. Kennedy, bought the property and put a finc addition onto the house and opened a private school. In 1843 Samuel B. Willet opened it as a house for the purpose of receiving boarders.

Not all taverns succumbed to the power of the Newtown Temperance Society, it seems. In an advertisement in the Bucks County *Intelligencer* in 1855, Jonathan Hibbs of the Whitehall Hotel seems to be throwing down the gauntlet when he titles an advertisement, "Prize Fight in Bucks County!"

> *Great Contest for the Championship, not as a Pugilist, but as a Saloon Keeper in Newtown.*
> *At the new and popular Establishment, corner of State and Mercer Streets, where the subscriber will keep constantly on hand all the Refreshments in the way of Eating and Drinking that are usually to be found in well conducted houses of this kind. Oysters and Clams served up in every style in their season, and Meals to Strangers at all reasonable hours. Connected with the above business, will be kept a choice lot of Wines and Liquors of all descriptions, at wholesale and retail, at reduced prices. Physicians and families purchasing for medical purposes, will find it to their advantage to buy at the Wine and Liquor Store, where they can procure better articles and upon more reasonable terms than elsewhere.*
> *Mind the place—corner of State and Mercer streets.*[33]

No longer used as a hotel, the Whitehall does have two restaurants on the first floor—Pat's Colonial Kitchen, which serves breakfast and lunch in a Victorian tearoom setting, and Duck Sauce, a Eurasian restaurant—with the rest of the building rented out as offices.

There are several more restaurants in Newtown that are located in historic buildings, and though nothing was found that would tell a story of historic events, they are special nonetheless. The Grotto (formerly Jean Pierre's) is located in a beautiful preserved stone building on State Street; Isaac Newtown's was originally the Newtown Academy; LaStalla Italian Restaurant is beautifully situated in the Lovett dairy barn; and 552 can be found in what was once the beautiful Victorian building called Lavender Hall.

Langhorne (Attleboro and Four Lanes End)

The area located midway between the river farms and those lands farther inland was called Middle Township, later shortened to Middletown, and the first mention of this vast area of land was in a report given at the Neshaminy Meeting House in 1692.

The first settlers to this part of Bucks County were two Dutch brothers named Abraham and Christian Van Horn. They settled about 1656, and built their log cabins just off the American Indian path that eventually became known as North Bellevue Avenue. There was an influx of English Quakers from 1678 to 1680, and they brought with them the concept of established towns that included a public house, a store and the artisans and tradesmen that were needed to form a proper settlement. By 1700, Four Lanes End in Middle Township indeed had a store, a blacksmith shop and a house of entertainment, and the log cabins were replaced by stone structures.

The White Hall Hotel's Victorian façade has changed very little since the early nineteenth century, even after a disastrous fire destroyed the interior in 1979. After restoration (inset), it became a home to offices and two restaurants. *Courtesy of the Newtown Historical Association.*

The Van Horns built the first inn, a small hipped-roof brick and stone house with a log kitchen attached, where the roads from Bristol to Durham and Trenton to Philadelphia intercepted—"major" roads that were still just widened Native American paths. Joseph Richardson built the first store in town at those same crossroads, which he and his wife, Mary Paxson, ran from the first floor of their large home. The archived ledgers show that the store was frequented by local settlers, American Indians and prominent men such as Benjamin Franklin and John Hancock.

Revolutionary War Graveyard

Newtown wasn't the only place that housed the Continental Army and Hessian soldiers the night after the Battle of Trenton. General Washington had designated Four Lanes End a military hospital immediately following the Battle of Trenton, and several buildings were taken over by the Continental Army.

On the night of December 26, a soldier came to the Richardson house and requested that the family clear as much of the house as they could for officers and soldiers, which they did, and the lower floor of the house was occupied by as many soldiers as could fit inside. The army surgeon was one of them. Isaac Hicks's house and tannery across the road were made into an infirmary, and the village—the only official army hospital in the area, although the Thompson-Neely house is said to have been a makeshift infirmary—was overtaken with soldiers, both sick and well.

Many of the soldiers encamped in Bucks County were seriously ill or were wounded in the battles that took place in quick succession that winter. We know of 166 of them that died, but there were likely many more than that. News of the military hospital must have spread, because there is an account of a man from Massachusetts who came to Four Lanes End to see his wounded son. The boy died, and the father left the infirmary and sat on a porch with a local resident, obviously needing to talk. He explained that six of his sons had now died in the war, and his youngest was getting ready to sign up. A parent can give nothing more precious or valuable than his sons to his country.

The daughter of Joseph Richardson, eleven-year-old Jane, witnessed the burial of the soldiers from an upper story window in her home. She watched as coffins were loaded onto sleds standing outside the Hicks house, then the sleds were drawn to the burial site down the road where the quickly constructed coffins were placed in shallow graves. These brave men, who gave their lives for the freedoms we often take for granted, were buried in a corner lot, three or four in a grave, at a makeshift graveyard approximately sixty-five feet by one hundred feet. Since the ground was frozen during what has been described as a bitter winter, the graves were shallow. But it is a credit to the people of Langhorne who took time to construct those many wooden caskets, as that was not always the case during the Revolution.

The army hospital remained in Four Lanes End until spring; this practice took place until May 1777 when the troops moved on. As the warm weather approached, dogs started to dig up the graves, and neighbors of the little graveyard hauled dirt in carts to mound over the area to protect the graves—and themselves from the odor. But there were no stones, no marker to signify the hallowed ground. Jane's account was recorded in an unpublished journal by her nephew Joshua Richardson in 1869, but it was thought of more as a legend than fact.

Then in 1992, when owners of the property had applied for subdivision of the tract of land where the Revolutionary War soldiers were supposed to have been buried that winter of 1776–1777, local residents protested. What if that corner really was a burial ground? The borough's planning commission and borough council hired Dr. R. Michael Steward of Temple University's Department of Anthropology to find evidence—just in case the story was true.

The archeological survey crew was given three days to find any proof that human remains were buried there. They returned each day without results. Just as they were about to give up, thinking that the story was a legend after all, they searched one more time near some shrubs. There, about a foot below the surface, they found a series of eighteenth-century handwrought rosehead nails, all lined up and pointing in the same direction, evenly spaced in the outline of a coffin. Digging deeper, they found several bone fragments and teeth. All in all, they determined that at least 166 soldiers were buried at that site. They did not, however, find a single button or piece of cloth—reflecting the fact that any uniforms or undergarments these soldiers may have had on when they fell ill or were wounded were reused by the ill-clad soldiers who were left to fight.

The soldiers buried in that quiet unmarked cemetery represent seven of the original thirteen colonies of the United States. The Woods Services, Inc, a school for disabled persons that owned the tract of land, dedicated it to Langhorne to be preserved forever. The residents of Langhorne take their responsibility very seriously, and the quiet little

During an archaeological survey in 1992, it was confirmed that at least 166 Continental Army soldiers were buried in unmarked graves in the winter/spring of 1776–77. The Langhorne site is now on the National Register of Historic Places. *Courtesy of Revolutionary War Site Commemoration Committee.*

corner of Flowers and Bellevue Avenue is kept immaculate. Today there is a marker and the American flag. Thanks to the citizens of Langhorne, these soldiers are no longer forgotten.

Four Lanes continued to be a major commercial center from the early eighteenth century to the mid-nineteenth century. Maple Avenue and Bellevue Avenue—a stretch of Durham Road—were at the heart of the village and several stagecoaches arrived and left from the crossroads daily, going east and west and north and south. Passengers could stay or eat at the local tavern and inn until they continued on their journey to their next destination.

When Gilbert Hicks, grandfather of the artist Edward Hicks, was discovered to be a Loyalist and his land was confiscated, it was sold in smaller lots, which brought even more settlers and businesses to the borough. Stores and craftsman shops spread along the roads that led in and out of the town.

The name of the village changed from Four Lanes End to Atleebury in 1737 and the borough became incorporated as Attleborough in December 1874. (There are numerous spellings that appear in documents, but one story claims that a man named

Langhorne was originally called Four Lanes End. The historic Langhorne Hotel can be seen on the far left. (Additional photos of the Langhorne Hotel can be seen in Chapter 3.) *Courtesy of Historic Langhorne Association.*

William Richardson Atlee was the principal contributor to the purchase of the first firetruck, and when it arrived the word "Atleebury" was painted on its side.)

When the railroad came to the area and needed to establish a station midway between Attleborough and Hulmeville, a great controversy arose when it wasn't clearly defined which town's name should be prominent at the station. The president of the railroad settled the argument by calling the station "Langhorne" since the tracks crossed Jeremiah Langhorne's former estate called Langhorne Park. Shortly after, Attleborough petitioned for a name change to Langhorne and received court approval—resulting, of course, in the station name being the same as the town's name.

In the late 1800s, when prosperous Philadelphians found they could reach Langhorne easily because of the Philadelphia and Bound Brook Railroad, and that the air in the lovely town was clear and healthful, they began to build large, elegant homes along South Bellevue Avenue, creating a Philadelphia suburb in the once quiet village. Houses with Victorian turrets and wraparound porches, surrounded by wrought-iron or picket fences, appeared beside the Federal-style brick houses or small frame and stone of the original inhabitants. The Langhorne Improvement Company realized that it was fashionable for Philadelphia suburbs to have a country club with a golf course, and so the Bucks County Country Club was established. The country club was a huge success, although the course itself left a lot to be desired since the first chairman of the

The Strawbridge family of Philadelphia frequented the Langhorne Hotel via their personal stagecoach. *Courtesy of Historic Langhorne Association.*

Greens Course had never played golf or even seen a golf course. It became the site of elegant dances, banquets and tournaments.

Underground Railroad

Although not exclusive to Langhorne, perhaps this is where we should explore the Underground Railroad in Bucks County. Bucks County was the "Fourth Road" in the escape route of slaves from the South. It ran steadily from 1840 to 1850. The mainline of escape through Pennsylvania was primarily by way of York, Adams, Lancaster and Chester counties, and the underground line through Bucks County was less used. Yet many slaves came through the county, reaching it through the Chester County line by way of Norristown or through Philadelphia.

In Samuel C. Eastburn's "Old Attleborough" article in the *Delaware Valley Advance* of 1929, he compares the steam railroad with the Underground Railroad, describing the latter "as unique in its methods."

> *Its right of way was by the public roads and many lanes and byways. Its stations were almost exactly ten miles apart. It ran but in one direction, always north. The North Star was its headlight. Its motive power was a pair of mules hitched to a closely covered wagon. Its conductors were plain faced but determined looking Quaker farmers. It ran only at night and without headlights.*[34]

In both Eastburn's article and in "A Collection of Papers Read Before the Bucks County Historical Society," which was a series of lectures given by Edward H. Magill to the historical society and later published in the *Friends Intelligencer*, the expression "North Star" was used to signify the guiding light toward which Southern refugees looked in their escape from bondage. For them, the light of the North Star was brightest in Canada, where they would find freedom. "Follow the Drinkin' Gourd" referred to the Big Dipper, which the fugitives would use to guide them on their northward journey.

The Quaker community was certainly not the only group to assist the escapees, but as passionate abolitionists, they accounted for a high number in the network of the railroad movement, especially in Pennsylvania. They acted as agents (to help slaves find the railroad); conductors (guides along the route); stationmasters (hiding slaves in their homes or barns); or stockholders (financiers who donated money for clothing and other needs).

They learned the code phrases, worked in the middle of the night to guide the fugitives from one station to another or to provide meals when they arrived at their homes and knew that by helping they were breaking the law. They were also aware that they were risking the freedom of their own African workers, for when the "slave catchers" came to the area to search for fugitives they often took free black citizens and sold them into slavery. Under the Fugitive Slave Law of 1850, suspected fugitives had no right to a jury trial and could not testify on their own behalf when brought before a magistrate. Many of the residents of Bucks County who were active in the railroad were silent about their work and brought as little attention to themselves as possible.

The railroad wasn't an easy route for the fugitives. They traveled in constant fear all night long and rested in hiding during the day. They believed that discovery was just around the next bend, at the next barn or in the next cellar. Yet, many started to feel more at ease when they reached Pennsylvania, and sometimes felt confident enough to stay in the towns and hamlets of Bucks County.

The Underground Railroad in Bucks County zigzagged to elude pursuit, but all accounts report that it started in Bristol, moved through Morrisville, Yardley, Langhorne, Newtown, Wrightstown, Buckingham, New Hope and almost always ended in Quakertown at the home of Richard Moore—the last important station of the Underground Railroad in Bucks County. From his home, Mr. Moore helped the courageous "passengers" follow the North Star beyond this county. All of these towns have evidence of the Underground Railroad, either in the basements of their churches, their taverns and inns, the barns and even in tunnels below the ground that connected one farm to another.

Tucked between major highways and hidden from the many shopping malls of the area, Langhorne Borough is still a small town where residents know each other's names. Walking down sidewalks brings back the charm of Americana. It is known for its public as well as private schools, numerous churches and is the home of St. Mary Medical Center, one of the largest and comprehensive acute care medical centers in the Philadelphia region.

The Langhorne Hotel

Although there was a tavern and inn in existence for many years at the center of Four Lanes End, the first license to serve liquor is dated 1724 when the Quarter Sessions Court of the Colonies granted the owner of the building a license to keep a "House of Entertainment." William Huddleston had expanded on the Van Horn's log and stone building and called it the Tavern at Attleboro. As mentioned, Four Lanes End was a hub for stagecoach lines. The first stagecoach was run by James Drake in 1738 and would leave Third Street in Philadelphia "before the rising sun" and arrive for breakfast at the Tavern at Attleboro on the route to New York.

When the town's name changed, so did the hotel's name. It passed through many hands over the following decades and several architectural changes took place. Originally a small two-and-a-half-story tavern with a peaked roof, by the late 1800s the tavern was three stories, had a second-floor porch and a flat roof. Outbuildings included a twenty-horse-stall livery stable and a two-story carriage house, which stored wagons, carriages and sleighs, and there was a row of double sheds for the horses and wagons for the hotel's transient guests. In front of the hotel was a hand pump topped with a wooden box that held cups so that people who passed could stop for a cool drink.

The Langhorne Hotel's fine reputation was known even in Philadelphia, and the Strawbridge family, of Strawbridge & Clothier, one of the largest and first department stores in Philadelphia, used to travel from Philadelphia in their personal coach, Tally Ho, to dine at the hotel.

When George G. Erhlen purchased the Langhorne Hotel in 1905, he understood the need to keep up with progress, while determined to keep the historical integrity of the building. He added a gas pump to fill the gas tanks of the few automobiles that were appearing on the surrounding roads. After World War I and with the advent of the Depression, many people moved away from Langhorne, which changed the community from a bustling progressive center of commerce back to a quiet hometown.

During World War II, the Federal Government Agency approached the Ehrlen estate to lease the property and turn it into apartments for workers in local war plants as there was a housing shortage at the time. After the war the building was returned to the owner and was subsequently sold to new owners, Harry and Wanda Force, who renovated the building and resumed serving food.

Since 1972, the hotel has remained under the ownership and management of the Asta family, who continue to run the business. The Langhorne Hotel has continuously served the community since the very beginning of the settlement's existence and it is still a busy center of social life.

Bridgetown Mill House

For more than 250 years, mills have had a decided importance in the endurance of an area. One of the most important in colonial America was the gristmill, which was used

An electric trolley line was built in Langhorne in 1894 and extended to Bristol, Newtown, Hulmeville, Wycombe and Doylestown. *Courtesy of Historic Langhorne Association.*

to grind grains such as wheat, rye, oat and barley into flour and meal. Almost every township in the colonies had a mill of some sort, whether it was a fulling mill to clean and dry wool, a gristmill or a sawmill for wood. Not long after an area was settled and a town was established, a mill was built.

Gristmills had the most importance and usually operated seasonally with the harvest. Custom mills ground grains individually for farmers and other individuals, and merchant mills were commercial milling operations that produced flour packaged into barrels for sale in stores or for export. Without the gristmills, many of the taverns and inns in Bucks County—or anywhere for that matter—couldn't provide the one important staple of every meal—bread—along with other essential food preparation supplies.

One of the early settlers of Bucks County, Thomas Jenks, built and operated a fulling mill that specialized in homespun goods. It was located along Core Creek in Middletown and was one of the first in Bucks County. Thomas Jenks was a prominent man, a well-respected Quaker, who served on the committee of observation before and during the Revolutionary War. One of his sons, also named Thomas, was to become even more well known and important in local and national politics. He served in the Colonial Assembly in 1773, the Constitutional Convention from 1789 to 1790 and in the state Senate from 1790 to 1799.

Thomas's son Joseph, on the other hand, followed in the family business. When Jonas Preston decided to sell his gristmill in Bucks County and establish one in Brandywine in Delaware, Joseph bought it. It was called the Bridgetown Mill and was also located on lush green acreage along the graceful Core Creek near the Bridgetown Pike that connected Langhorne and Newtown with Feasterville.

George Erhlen purchased the Langhorne Hotel in 1905 and managed it through Prohibition when he was forced to serve oysters and ice cream from the historic tavern instead of spirited beverages. *Courtesy of Historic Langhorne Association.*

Joseph was a major agriculturist and established a fifty-one-acre tract adjacent to Bridgetown that he called Edgewood where he could practice his farming skills. All at one time, Joseph operated his gristmill, his father's fulling mill and his gentleman's farm—with success. In 1791, he built a stunning stone mansion house near the mill, which was referred to as the Bridgetown Mill House.

When he died, he left the property to his son, who in turn left the estate to his own sons, Charles and Joseph. Charles built a home for himself and his family on Edgemont while Joseph remained at the Bridgetown Mill House and ran the gristmill until the 1840s. He operated it as a merchant mill and amassed considerable wealth. He sold the mill and house to Samuel Comfort in 1847, and in 1876 the property was purchased by Benjamin Woodman. It remained in the Woodman family until 1953. The mill continued to operate until 1939, but since then the building has deteriorated, although its former splendor is evident and adorns the property of what is now the Bridgetown Mill House Bed and Breakfast.

For years, Carlos and Kim DaCosta passed the Bridgetown Mill property on their way to work, and dreamed that one day they would own it and turn it into a restaurant and inn. When the property became available, their dream came true. The DaCostas carefully renovated and decorated each bedroom with period furniture, named the rooms for the many varieties of trees that grow on the property—Sycamore, Maple, Walnut and Magnolia—and turned the third floor into their private residence.

Although the gristmill is not much more than a shell of what it once was, a renovation is being considered for the future.

Northampton and Southampton

Buck Hotel, Black Bear Tavern and White Bear Tavern

Southampton and Northampton were quiet farming communities in the west of Bucks County bordering Philadelphia and Montgomery County. Unlike the towns along Durham Road, these townships counted more churches and religious organizations than hostelries. However, there were a few taverns and inns that were extremely popular: the Buck Hotel, the Black Bear Tavern and the White Bear Tavern, which later became the Spread Eagle Inn.

These taverns were the settings for numerous political meetings, but one of particular note concerns African American suffrage. For several years African Americans in Bucks County enjoyed the same voting rights as Caucasians did, but when the Democrats who controlled Bucks County were defeated in the 1837 election, they asserted that it was due to "illegal" black votes. What ensued afterwards resulted in a change in African American suffrage for the entire Commonwealth of Pennsylvania.

During 1837, a constitutional convention was taking place in Philadelphia, and one of the amendments being discussed was voting privileges. The state constitution stated, "In elections by citizens, every freeman of the age 21 years and upward who has resided in the state one year preceding such election shall be entitled to vote in the county or district in which he shall reside."[35] There was no mention of race. African Americans assumed that this meant anyone who was not a slave or servant and who met all voter qualifications. John Sterigere, a Montgomery County Democrat, disagreed and proposed that the word "white" be inserted before "freeman." Phineas Jenks of Bucks County argued vehemently against Sterigere, stating that there were wealthy black property owners living in Bucks County that were qualified and had the right to vote. And so the debate in Philadelphia continued, with Democrats, Whigs and Anti-Masons from across the state all taking sides for and against.

Then on October 10, 1837, an election to fill six Bucks County vacancies was held, and the Democrats who had been in control lost by slim margins. They contested the results, claiming that they lost because twenty-four black men who did not have the right to vote arrived at polls with loaded guns threatening that anyone who tried to stop them from voting would be shot. Two important facts in this story were ignored: no one was certain that the "illegal" black men who were named even voted, and it was the first day of hunting season when most men would be carrying guns with the intent to hunt after casting their vote.

Citizens, politicians and lawyers on both sides met at the Black Bear Tavern to argue the issue. During a series of three meetings held at the Black Bear, the White Bear and the Buck Tavern in Nockamixon, the Democrats drew up petitions that were submitted to the state legislature, the constitutional convention and the county court in Doylestown requesting that the right to vote be limited to *white* freemen.

Bridgetown Mill House was one of the most distinctive homes in Bucks. Although the mill has fallen into ruin, the present owners are considering restoration. It also is said to have been a station on the Underground Railroad. *Courtesy of Bridgetown Mill House Bed and Breakfast.*

Their arguments must have been persuasive, if misguided, because African Americans in Pennsylvania lost their voting privileges not only in Bucks County but throughout Pennsylvania until the passage of the Fourteenth Amendment of the United States Constitution in 1868. This is a perfect example of how important political issues—issues that affected the lives of citizens—were determined in the taverns of America.

The Black Bear Tavern burned down and is no longer in existence. The Spread Eagle Inn (White Bear) continued to operate as a restaurant until the 1990s, and is now an office building. The Buck Hotel remains one of the most popular and well-known establishments in Bucks County and surrounding areas.

The Spread Eagle Inn, originally the White Bear Tavern, was built in the eighteenth century and was saved from demolition in 2001 when local residents raised enough funds to cover the cost of moving the building. *Author Collection.*

Wrightstown Township

Pineville Tavern

Durham Road, sometimes called the "great road" was the only continuous road connecting the southern and northern portions of Bucks County. Such an important road would boast many taverns, stagecoach stops and inns. It connected Bristol to Newtown, then Wrightstown through "the Pines" (Pineville) to Buckingham and finally to the Durham Forge in Easton.

Pennsylvania agriculture has always been diverse. Beef, pork, dairy animals and dairy products were major agricultural products, as were crops such as grain, tobacco, garden vegetables and a wide variety of fruit. From the earliest days of Colonial Pennsylvania, farmers raised a variety of plants and animals for their own consumption and for barter and sale. In addition to taking their wares to major towns and ports, sales and auctions of livestock, farm equipment and land took place from the yards of numerous taverns.

In Bucks County, the Pineville Tavern, located on Durham Road in Wrightstown Township, was well known for lively auctions and barter. The Pineville Tavern, built

Pineville Tavern originally was a drover's stop where livestock and an assortment of goods were auctioned from the front porch. *Courtesy of the Pineville Tavern.*

in 1742, was located in the center of the hamlet and was opened first as a temperance house. After receiving a license to serve liquor, the tavern grew even more popular and ultimately became the center of "business" among farmers, wagoners and drovers.

Today it remains one of the most popular restaurants and taverns in Bucks County. The owner, Andrew Abruzzese, is meticulous in keeping the rustic charm and integrity of the establishment. It is truly like stepping back in time whenever one enters the tavern room at the front of the building, and the backroom retains its historical charm with exposed beams and what was once a large kitchen hearth.

Pipersville
Historic Piper Tavern

Never let it be said that women weren't as courageous or as patriotic as the men, and as the call to arms was directed towards men, many women fought beside their husbands, brothers and sons, and even donned the uniform of the Continental Army. They assisted in cleaning the rifles, loading the cannons, mending the soldiers' clothes and nursing the sick and wounded in the camps. Some even acted as spies, and others took up arms and fought on the front lines.

Eva Lear Piper was the daughter of Tobias Lear, the private secretary to General George Washington. She was a dedicated patriot, and the tavern she owned with her husband, George, was a well-known gathering place for anyone who wanted to discuss the cause for liberty. Some of their guests were Benjamin Franklin, Generals Wayne and LaFayette and several signers of the Declaration of Independence. Loyalists, on the other hand, were unwelcome. Not surprisingly, George Piper joined the Continental Army at the outbreak of the war, as did three of their six children, and left his wife to operate the large Piper's Tavern.

Perhaps one of the stories for which Eva is best known is the "battle" she fought in her own tavern. She was ironing one day during the war when two members of the notorious Loyalist gang run by the Doan brothers stormed into the inn, and it was obvious they were up to trouble. Without hesitating, Eva threw her hot iron at one of the outlaws, a man named Geddis, and broke his arm below the shoulder. His accomplice, Gibson, tried to strike her with his whip, but Eva grabbed her husband's sword and drove the outlaws from her property. Geddis's arm was in such bad shape he was unable to mount his horse and was forced to walk miles before he could find a physician to set the arm. And although that story speaks of her courage, another tells of her compassion and conviction. When Colonel Piper came home during the war to try and raise money for desperately needed shoes and clothing for the troops under his command, Eva gave him her entire inheritance of gold, which she had buried in a crock in the cellar of the tavern. It was enough to fill two saddlebags and purchase enough clothes and boots to keep his men from freezing in the cold winter months.

The town in which this tavern is located was officially named Pipersville in 1845 in honor of the colonel and his courageous wife.

Doylestown

For many years after Penn established his colony, the place in Bucks County that is called Doylestown had only a few small log homes scattered amidst very heavily forested lands that originally belonged to the Free Society of Traders. The Free Society of Traders was established in Philadelphia in 1682 as a monopoly intended to handle fur trade with the American Indians, produce linen and wine for export and set up glass factories. The organization was also supposed to dig iron and lead mines and fish for whales, but it collapsed into bankruptcy in 1686 as it couldn't meet all of its goals.

Even after two main roads were built and crossed in what is now the heart of Doylestown, the area remained a wilderness. Brothers Edward and William Doyle were the earliest settlers and purchased much of the land adjacent to the crossroads where they built the first tavern. In the petition for a license in 1745 it is stated that there were no other taverns within five miles of the crossroads—testimony to the fact that it was still mostly backwoods since taverns could be found in Bucks County just about every mile in the lower part of the county.

Eventually, when it became known that it was strategically located at the crossroads of routes that linked Norristown with Coryell's Ferry (New Hope) and Philadelphia with Easton (State and Main Streets), the tiny hamlet around Doyle's tavern grew into a village. Families looking for land started to settle in the area, and more taverns and hotels were built.

The Piper Tavern was a favorite meeting spot for members of the Continental Congress and officers of the Continental Army, who were welcomed by George and Eva Piper. Eva was the daughter of Tobias Lear, George Washington's secretary. *Courtesy of Piper Tavern.*

In 1773, the Flack family owned a tavern called The Ship. A heartbreaking story around that tavern concerns a child of Samuel Flack who died in the family's quarters of the tavern. It appears that on the day she was to be buried, May 1, 1778, a rather violent battle between the Continental Army and the British was taking place at Crooked Billet (Hatboro). None would leave their homes, in fear that they'd get caught between the two armies as they approached the town. Four people, two men and two women, left the tavern with the body of the child in a coffin. They hurriedly mounted horses, and with one of the men holding the coffin across his saddle, they galloped to the burial ground to quickly lay the child to rest. The sound of gunfire and cannons grew closer to the town as the Pennsylvania militia under the command of Brigadier General John Lacey was retreating from the attack by the British. The women didn't dismount in fear that they would need to flee quickly from the British. Once the sad little funeral was finished, all four retreated quickly back to safety of The Ship. Only one person in the funeral procession is identified in both Davis's and Battle's accounts. She was a neighbor of the Flacks. The others are unknown, but we have to hope that at least one parent was a member of the hasty funeral procession that buried the tiny child.

When county settlements grew north, Doylestown replaced Newtown as a central location and became the third and present county seat of Bucks. After the establishment of a courthouse in 1813, a line of Federal-style buildings called "lawyers

Doyle's Tavern was originally built in 1757, and within a few years was surrounded by several hospitality establishments. In 1902, two buildings were combined to make a larger hotel, which still houses visitors coming to the county seat. *Courtesy of Doylestown Inn.*

row" was developed. Large tracts of land were subdivided and residential lots provided room for wealthy homes.

Since there was no strong water power in the village, Doylestown was able to remain a more professional and residential center and avoided industrial development. But the bulk of expansion took place after the Civil War, when Doylestown boasted gas lights, an electric telegraph station and became a stop on the branch of the North Pennsylvania Railroad.

When it became the county seat, taverns and hotels were essential to the town in order to refresh and house the numerous lawyers, politicians and visitors to court. The Fountain House, which was built in 1804, is believed to have been built on the same site where William Doyle's original tavern was located. It was the premier hotel of its time, a favorite of the lawyers and politicians at court. Its grand presence remains in the center of town, although not as a hotel.

Other noted hotels in Doylestown were the Indian Queen Tavern, the Cross Keys Tavern, the Clear Spring Hotel, and the Citizen's House; but today, the only lodging that remains in the historic section of Doylestown is the Doylestown Inn, which was established in 1902. It sits at the heart of the borough and operates as a bed-and-breakfast, offering the quiet charm of yesteryear.

During the Civil War, Fort Lacey was the post of the Doylestown Guard and of the 104th Regiment of Pennsylvania Volunteers. Both were organized under Captain W.W.H. Davis, the author of the *History of Bucks County, Pennsylvania*. Davis and his Doylestown Guards were the first Bucks County volunteers to fight for the Union Cause. They were part of the advance guard marching on Richmond at Fair Oaks. Bucks County cherishes the part its citizens played in the Civil War, and Doylestown houses the Civil War Roundtable and Museum to promote the study of this important event in American history.

Doylestown is the cultural center of Bucks County, with four major museums within walking distance of each other, including the Mercer Museum, Fonthill and the James A. Michener Art Museum. In 2001, Doylestown was listed on the National Trust for Historic Preservation as one of its "Distinctive Destinations," and is listed on the National Register of Historic Places thanks to the Bucks County Redevelopment Authority, which was formed to protect the historical integrity of the city.

Part III

The “Stone Coal” Waterway

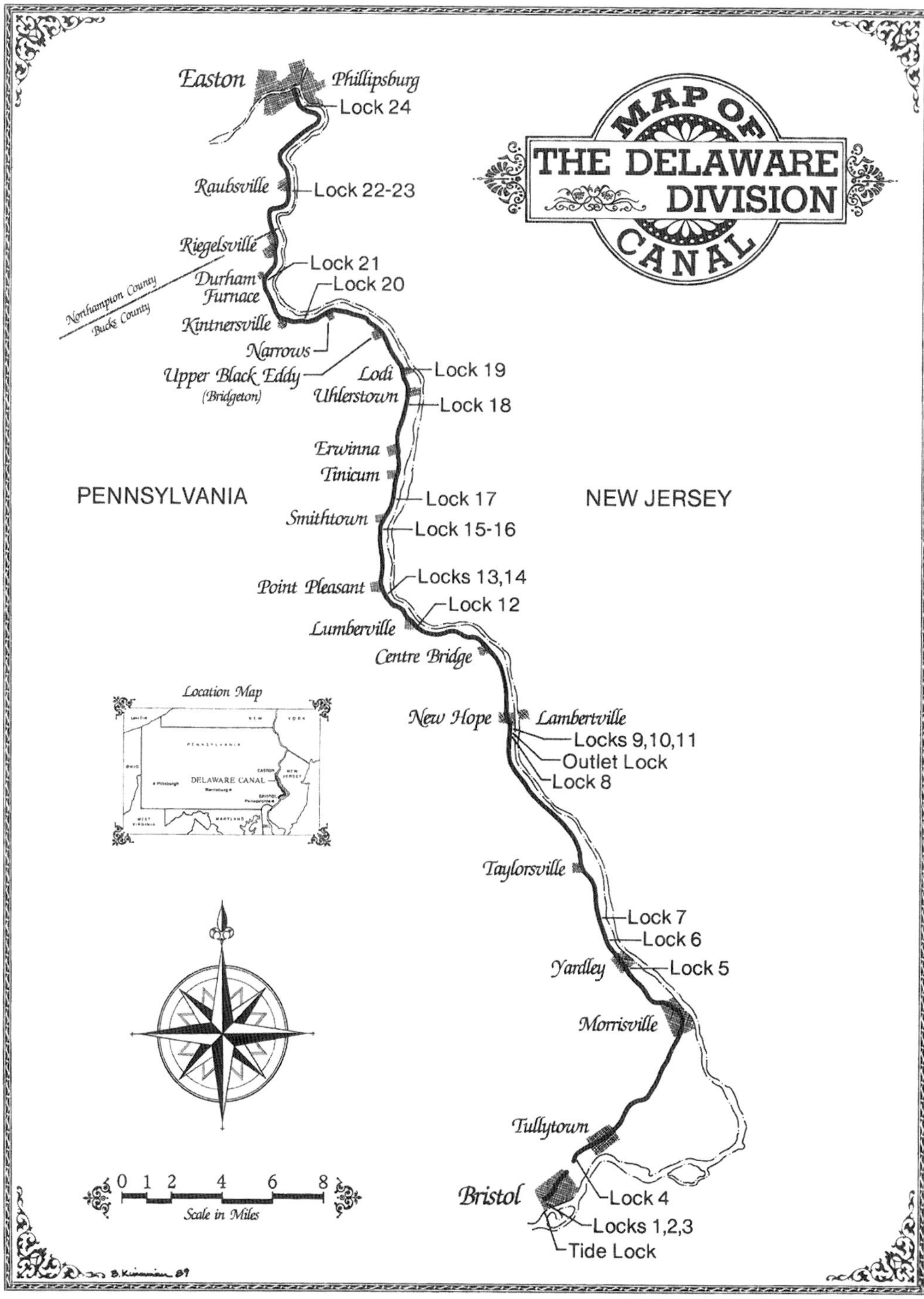

Courtesy of the Pennsylvania Canal Society Collection, National Canal Museum, Easton, PA.

Chapter 6

The Era of Snappers and Stiff Boats

Be not forgetful to entertain strangers, For thereby some have entertained angels unawares.
—Hebrews 13:2

*A delicate, fragile ribbon of water…an engineering marvel…a stone coal turnpike…*These are all images used in describing the canal that was carved through the land beside the Delaware River from Mauch Chunk (Jim Thorpe) in the northeast mountains of Pennsylvania to Bristol at Pennsylvania's southeast end. And it's true, the Lehigh Navigation and Delaware Division Canal are all of those things—delicate and fragile, an engineering marvel with its locks and aqueducts, a turnpike that marked an era of industrial progress in early America—and it was also a way of life for Pennsylvanians for more than ninety-seven years.

Couples began their married lives on the canal, children were born on the canal and others lost their lives on it. The canal is yet another example of the multicultural richness of this country, where people of different races, nationalities and economic situations worked together to make the canal system a thriving mode of commerce. The canal's history is not only intertwined in the history of our nation, but also of its populace.

When it was discovered that the Lehigh Valley's clean, slow burning stone coal could not be overlooked as a viable multiuse fuel, venture capital poured into the region's mountains—along with Pennsylvania's daring sons—and the Lehigh Coal Mines Company was formed. The anthracite coal was as important to industry in America as it was to heating America's homes.

After being mined from the bowels of the mountains, the anthracite coal had to be transported to Philadelphia and New York, and points between. At first, the coal was transported from the mountains downriver in arks; however, the rivers were unpredictable—one day calm and slow-flowing, the next raging—and the arks were caught up in the wild currents and either smashed against the rocks or grounded on the banks of the river.

To manage this problem, an extensive canal system in Pennsylvania was developed and divided into two sections: the Lehigh Navigation and the Delaware Division. The sixty-mile Delaware Canal was dug and built by local farmers and Irish immigrants using picks, shovels and wheelbarrows, who were paid seventy-five cents a day—no matter how many hours a day they worked. It took from 1827 to 1832 to complete the forty-foot wide and seven-foot deep channel, which ran from Bristol to Easton, where it then turned into the Lehigh Navigation. The entire system cost $1,400,000 to build.

The canal employed a series of hydrostatic locks—also called bear traps—that would create an "artificial flood" that changed water levels, allowing the barges to flow freely in either direction. Since this type of engineering was new to the region, and the laborers inexperienced in canal building, it was completed by trial and error, with the engineers learning from their mistakes as they went along.

Eventually, it proved to be an expedient way to transport heavy cargo, and in addition to coal mined from the mountains, the barges also carried lumber, building stone, lime, produce and Bushkill whiskey. On return trips, the barges carried manufactured or imported goods.

The people made the canal work, from the engineers, who were called upon constantly to rebuild and maintain portions washed away by floods from the river and cascades of water from the hillsides, to the lock tenders, who were crucial in keeping the barges moving along, and the barge captains and mule drivers, who made the transportation of heavy loads seem easy. *Seem* is the operative word, for working on the canal was anything but easy.

Men, women and children worked the mule-driven canal boats or the locks, and the days were long and hard. They would often start at four o'clock in the morning and didn't stop until around ten o'clock at night when the lock tenders stopped work, but rest didn't come until the mules were unharnessed, brushed and fed. Carrying anywhere from 80 tons to 112 tons of cargo, the canal boats moved approximately thirty miles a day—two miles an hour when full and four miles an hour when empty, and required a crew of at least two people, one to steer the barge and one to drive the mules. Once on the route, they avoided any stops along the way and cooked and slept onboard. The mule drivers pole-vaulted from the towpath to the deck in order to eat or rest without stopping the mules, which meant that a well-trained team of mules was invaluable.

Most boatmen, and sometimes their families, lived on their boats all year, even during the cold winter months when the canals were drained for maintenance. Babies were born in the tiny eight- by ten-foot cabins, which were only large enough to hold a stove and two bunk beds. To the canal men, the barges were their lives' work, and their mules were almost as important as their children. They were Irish, German and African American, and they were rough around the edges. Some played music and sang to keep themselves entertained on the long, dreary trips up and down the canal; others picked fights.

Time was money for the bargemen and their families. They traveled in the dark, hanging a "night hawk" lantern on the bow to light their way. They walked the towpath and steered the barge without protection in rain, sleet, snow and hundred-degree temperatures. They announced their approach to the lock tenders by blowing into a conch shell or trumpet, anxious to get through the lock as quickly as possible without losing time. The barges could measure eighty-seven feet, ten feet wide and seven feet deep, and some came in two sections, called hinge boats or "snappers." Single barges were called stiff boats. Men as old as seventy-two years and boys as young as sixteen captained the barges—the only qualification they needed to gain that rank was to skillfully navigate a hinge boat through an aqueduct. They were paid $27 a month, and it took around forty-eight hours to travel from Easton to Bristol. Many of the mule drivers were barefoot boys or girls as young as eight years old, walking sixty miles in two days one way, then turning around and doing the same back up the canal. Their only rest was in January and February when the canal was empty, and even then, many of the bargemen worked with the crews who repaired the damaged canal during the winter.

Life wasn't much easier for the lock tenders, who worked from four o'clock in the morning to ten o'clock at night, six days a week, and lived in tiny houses by the side of the canal, which were built buy the "Company." In order to make ends meet, many of the women in the lock tender houses sold baked goods to the boatmen, prepared food and took in their wash, along with raising livestock, tending their crops and raising their children.

In the years before the Civil War, along with coal, lumber and pig iron, human "cargo" was sometimes hidden in the bottom of the barges; these were dark hiding places for escaping slaves. A light in the window of a home or designated inn along the canal would signal that an underground station was a safe, albeit temporary, refuge, and the terrified and exhausted fugitives climbed the canal berm and ran for cover at these compassionate sanctuaries.

And along the course of the canal, taverns and inns provided the most rudimentary form of refreshment and rest. In time, as the canal became popular for "leisure" cruises, these hostelries expanded and became more refined. They usually offered beautiful views of the quiet canal and gentle breezes from the Delaware River. As canal transportation was squeezed out by the railroads, many of these taverns and inns closed, but others became favored by city residents who found the river and canal superb for vacations in the warmer months.

The Towns and Inns along the Canal

Locks 1 to 7—Bristol to Yardley

Upon unloading their cargo at the terminus in Bristol, the barges turned around and moved up through the more industrial areas of the county until they reached the quiet, rural countryside. The Closson House, later known as the Keystone Hotel, was located on the Delaware Canal near where the canal let out into the river. It was frequented by the boatmen who had just brought their heavily laden barges to Bristol and were waiting for the coal to be transferred to the steamers that would bring it farther down the Delaware to the city of Philadelphia. After a brief respite at the Closson, they could hook up their mules to bring the empty—or lighter—barge back up the canal.

By the time they arrived at the lock at Yardley, the boatmen would be ready for refreshments before moving farther up the canal. The Continental Hotel and the White

Tolls were collected at the tide lock in Bristol and again in New Hope. Industrial buildings and mills were built along the edge of the canal as seen in the background. *Courtesy of the Pennsylvania Canal Society Collection, National Canal Museum, Easton, Pennsylvania.*

Swan (Yardley Inn) were prominent river and canal establishments. The Continental was one of the safe stations along the canal for escaping slaves.

William Yardley, one of William Penn's closest friends, was the first settler in the area, but when he and his family died in a smallpox epidemic in 1702, William's nephew Thomas came from England to settle the family's estate. Thomas expanded on the Yardley estate and purchased five hundred acres from Thomas Lambert, land which had a gristmill, millpond, millraces, millstones and edifices. He also established a ferry in Yardley in 1722, and erected a ferry house and tavern.

The White Swan, now called the Yardley Inn, was built by a man named Grear and replaced the original ferry house in Yardley, which had been washed away by one of the destructive floods common to the area.

River town communities subjected to floods know how to survive. They pump out the floodwater, and restore and rebuild—not just their own property and businesses, but each other's as well. Regardless of the hardships the Yardley Inn has endured over the years due to flooding, it remains a constant in town. Located between the river and the canal, archived photos from every generation show the floodwaters that have ravaged the building from both sides, and still it stands. According to Bob Freed, who with his wife Robin owns and operates the inn today, the residents of Yardley seem to will the building to survive. "During the floods, the local residents take care of us just as they do each other. Their concerns extend even to the restaurant." After every flood, the Yardley Inn cleans

The lock at Yardley is likely one of the sites where escaping slaves, hidden at the bottom of the canal boats, ran to the Continental Tavern for refuge until a "conductor" led them to the next "station." *Courtesy of the Pennsylvania Canal Society Collection, National Canal Museum, Easton, Pennsylvania.*

up, recoups and opens its doors again. The barroom fills with patrons, and the restaurant hums with the voices of the locals who treat the restaurant as though it is their home away from home.

Floods along the Delaware are notorious, and when unexpected heavy rains cause flash floods, the water can rise higher than twenty feet in hours. During the height of the canal years, when forecasting weather was an unsophisticated science, floods during the nineteenth century washed away the canal banks and sometimes the barges—at times with the mules and drivers still holding on.

Locks 8 to 11—Yardley to New Hope

New Hope was a quiet little river village that was not much more than a small ferry point along the River Road. It was an important strategic point during the first few years of the Revolutionary War and was one of the encampments in December 1776 and in subsequent months. In fact, the British had entertained the idea of crossing into Pennsylvania at New Hope (then Coryell's Ferry) that December, but decided against it when the river wasn't frozen over and all the boats on the New Jersey side had been hidden or destroyed. Had they done so, there may have been a very different conclusion to the War for Independence.

There was an inn located at Coryell's Ferry, which was used by officers and soldiers in the Continental Army, one of them General George Washington, who signed the register a total of six times during the war years, and another General Benedict Arnold,

Despite numerous and disastrous floods over the last two hundred years, the Yardley Inn survives and remains rooted in the community as a favorite restaurant and meeting spot. *Courtesy of the Yardley Inn.*

who was headquartered there in the summer of 1777. A letter from General Arnold to General Washington was found in New Hope in June 1955, and the letter was published in its entirety by the *New Hope Gazette*. It read:

> *Coryells Ferry*
> *June 15, 1777*
> *5 O'Clock*
>
> *Dear General:*
> *I have rec'd no intelligence from Gen. Washington since 4 o'clk last evening, at which time the enemy were encamped at Sommersett Court House, under the command of Generals Howe and Cornwallis...The militia turn out in great numbers in the Jersies, Gen. Sullivan has gone to Flemingtown twelve miles from this, the Troops who arrive here are immediately sent after him, I am very fearful the enemy will retire to Brunswick before you arrive with your reinforcements, and oblige us to attack them at a disadvantage for fight them we must, when all our reinforcements are in we cannot avoid it with HONOR. Our men are in high spirits and in four days we shall have upwards of twenty thousand men.*

The Logan Inn was the headquarters of General Benedict Arnold during the summer of 1777, and before the Civil War served as a station in the Underground Railroad. *Courtesy of New Hope Historical Society.*

> *General Putnam has 8,000 men with him, Gen. Washington wrote three Days since for 4,000 to be sent him immediately. Many of the militia have little Ammunition, the cartredges sent to Bristol will soon be exhausted. It will be necessary to send here one thousand Cartredges sorted. A Quarter Master is also wanted. Gen. Sullivan has joynd him. No person is now here fit for the purpose.*
>
> *I expect every minute to hear from our Army & the Enemy. Every intelligence of consequence shall be forwarded to you directly.*
>
> *I am Dr. Gen Yours B. Arnold*

Shortly after this letter was written, Arnold was passed over for a promotion by Congress, even though he had distinguished himself in battle and was injured in the Saratoga campaign in New York in October. Bitter and in debt, Arnold arranged to be given command of West Point in July 1780 and while there, he plotted with the British to turn West Point over to them for twenty thousand pounds. His deception was discovered, and he was forced to escape to a British ship. The British made him a brigadier general, and he fought with them for the duration of the Revolution. After the war, he moved to London, but on both sides of the Atlantic he will be forever known as a traitor.

This bird's-eye view of the Delaware Canal focuses on Lock 11 in New Hope, which is now the headquarters for the Friends of the Delaware Canal. *Courtesy of New Hope Historical Society.*

When merchant Benjamin Parry's Hope Mills burned to the ground at Coryell's Ferry, he rebuilt and changed the name of his business to the New Hope Mills and the town adopted the name. About one hundred years after it was licensed, the hotel's name was changed to the Logan Inn in commemoration of the Lenape American Indian, Chief Wingohocking, who had exchanged his name for James Logan's—William Penn's secretary—whom he considered his friend. A metal cutout of a Native American with bow and arrow was placed on top of the inn. It is now on display on the Parry Mansion property. Pre-Civil War, the Logan Inn served as a station in the Underground Railroad.

When the Delaware Division Canal ran through the town, four of the locks were located within the current borough, with an outlet to the Delaware River where barges could cross the river to the Raritan Canal in New Jersey. The Lehigh Coal and Navigation Company built several buildings in New Hope as it was a central location along the route; these buildings included lock houses, tollhouses, a market and company offices. They also kept a boatyard in the borough for repairs and dry-dock. And bargemen could get some "comfort" at the Bucket of Blood brothel, if they were so inclined. In the 1860s, one hundred canal boats passed through New Hope each day.

Canal just south of Odette's in New Hope. Although closed after the flood of 2006, there are plans to reopen this historic canal-side restaurant. *Courtesy of New Hope Historical Society.*

The River House (Chez Odettes) was built in 1794, and is located at the lower end of the New Hope locks on the canal. At this point, barges could cross the river and connect with the Raritan Canal system in Lambertville, New Jersey. Tolls were collected here, and the amounts depended upon the cargo that was being carried along the canal.

During the canal years, New Hope was a bustling village that demonstrated a mixture of the Quaker's "plain living," the bargeman's edginess and the artist's soul. In the late nineteenth century, New Hope became a home for artists who loved its stone structures and lovely canal views. These artists, a group of inspired men and women, who were to become known as America's greatest impressionists, found the rural quiet, the beauty of nature and early Pennsylvania architecture perfect "subjects" for their paintings. Edward W. Redfield, Daniel Garber, Emasita Register Corson, Fern Isabel Coppedge and William I. Lathrop all settled in or near New Hope for a time and painted their landscapes and street scenes in all seasons, even tying their canvases to the trees in order to capture the beauty of a winter storm. The canal and the buildings along the water have been immortalized in their work. Quieter now than it was during the canal years, New Hope is still a center of culture and art in Bucks County, and its surrounding beauty can still take an artist's breath away. The taverns and inns that the New Hope impressionists painted in the nineteenth and early twentieth centuries are still being painted by artists today.

The Center Bridge Inn continues to offer respite to weary travelers—inside and on canal barges built and operated to keep the history of the canal alive. *Courtesy of Center Bridge Inn and New Hope Canal Boat Company.*

Just outside of New Hope borough, at the entrance to the Centre Bridge that spans the Delaware, a building once called Mitchell's Ferry (Centre Bridge Inn) perches on the banks of the Delaware overlooking the canal. When the Mitchell family built the structure, they took advice from the Lenape American Indians who knew the Delaware River well and who showed them exactly where to build the ferry house a safe distance from the flood areas for which the river was known. It was a wise move, and since 1705 the building has never experienced damage from flooding. When the bridge was built in 1814, families going to church and funeral processions could cross for free, but everyone else paid a toll to the innkeeper.

The bridge brought greater activity than the area had experienced before, and as a result the inn needed an icehouse, blacksmith shop and a stable. Although not considered a major stop on the canal since there were no locks at the location, the lower level of the Center Bridge Inn displays the original fireplace where food was cooked for patrons, and likely where the less affluent guests slept at night on its hearth. In 1903, the Centre Bridge was the only building left standing in town after a major flood. However, it was not invincible because on Halloween night in 1932, the Centre Bridge Inn caught fire. It was left in ruins for more than twenty years. In the 1950s it was rebuilt, but burned down again. Then in 1962, the Center Bridge Inn was restored to resemble the inn as it looked in the 1800s. Today it is a wedding destination, with brides coming to the inn from all parts of the world, and it remains a favorite vacation spot for families as well.

It cannot be said that Washington slept at the Black Bass, as it was a nucleus for Tory activities during the Revolution. It can be said that canal men were always welcome, however. *Courtesy of Black Bass Hotel.*

Not long after Tina and Jerry Horan purchased the Centre Bridge Inn, they purchased the lease to run the New Hope Canal Boat Company. The recreated barges take passengers on a ride down the canal, drawn by mule teams (Dot, Dolly, Joe and Daffodil) and narrated by canal boat Captain Dave and his mule driver Charles, who tell the story of life on the canal in the nineteenth century. Believing that the history of the canal should be kept alive, they have worked diligently after three major floods in the last several years to repair and maintain the canal, working in partnership with the Delaware Canal State Park.

Locks 12 to 24—Lumberville to Easton

On its website (www.blackbasshotel.com), the Black Bass Hotel (once the Lumberville House) claims that it was built "as a fortified haven for river travelers in the turbulent days of the 1740s when hostile American Indian bands roamed the forests." Located in Lumberville along the canal, it was also a haven for the bargemen who knew they would receive a first-class meal and entertainment on their journey along the canal. It also served the lumberjacks who cut down virgin trees, floated them to the city and worked in the local lumber mills. President Grover Cleveland used the hotel as a retreat, relishing the solitude and good fishing. As for the Revolution, this hostelry belonged to a Loyalist and Washington decidedly did not sleep or eat there. It would have been avoided by the Continental Army in fear that intelligence about their plans and schemes would have been related to the British.

Jimmy Brown, one of the last men to work the canal, walks the towpath beside Jacob Oberacker's taproom. *Courtesy of the Pennsylvania Canal Society Collection, National Canal Museum, Easton, Pennsylvania.*

During an especially raucous Saturday night when the bargemen and locals were busy partying, a fire broke out almost without notice. The proprietor at the time, Major Anthony Fry, realizing that the canal company had stored blasting powder in the cellar of his inn, broke down the door during the fire, grabbed the entire quantity of blasting powder and was able to leave the building unharmed. The fire was put out without too much harm to the building, and thanks to his actions the Black Bass continues to serve guests today and is a renowned bed-and-breakfast that hosts guests from all over the world.

The Golden Pheasant Inn was originally called the Delaware House and was built in 1857. During the canal years, it was operated by Jacob Oberacker, and bargemen stopped for a change of mules, beer, salt cakes (very like soft pretzels) and a bed for the night. Barbara and Michel Faure and their family have owned the historic building for over twenty-one years, and the beauty of the canal that runs behind it is as lovely as it was one hundred years ago. The Golden Pheasant is on the National Registry of Historic Places and is the longest continuously run mule barge stop on the canal.

There were several locks and taverns along the canal above Erwinna. Perhaps the most industrious town was Riegelsville, where John Riegel built and operated the Riegel Paper Company. Other factories and mills spread along the little hamlet's banks and company executives built mansions overlooking the canal and river. The Riegelsville Inn still serves the community as it did in the 1800s.

Now called the Golden Pheasant Inn, the building hasn't changed much, with entrances from both River Road and the towpath. It was a favorite stop for pleasure boaters on the canal. *Courtesy of Golden Pheasant Inn.*

The End of an Era

During the peak years of the Delaware Canal, the railroads were also being organized. Rails were laid in all directions, bigger and better steam engines were built and the railroad began to compete with the canal for freight transportation. The state sold the Delaware Division to the Lehigh Canal and Navigation Company, even as the company started to ship more of its coal by train. In 1866, 792,000 tons—1.5 billion pounds—of coal were pulled on the canal. In 1915, that number was reduced to 130,000 tons, and by 1931, only 65,000 tons went through the canal.[36] Oil replaced coal as a source of heat, and by the early twentieth century, truck deliveries were available. Bargemen's salaries decreased from $25 a month to $18 a month. In order to survive, they left the canals—for most of them a lifelong occupation—and sought work elsewhere. Lock tenders also lost their livelihood.

As fewer barges navigated the canal, pleasure boating on the Delaware Canal became a popular pastime in the late nineteenth century, and usually consisted of a party of several passengers that boarded a custom-built boat called a "packet" drawn by a mule. They spent several days boating from Bristol to Easton, with stops at elegant inns along the way. But pleasure boating couldn't offer the economics needed to sustain the canal.

When the railroads became the primary transportation system for anthracite coal, Pennsylvania discontinued the canal system. It is now the Delaware Canal State Park, a National Historic Landmark. *Author Collection.*

Residents of Bucks and Northampton counties cherished the historic canal, and they formed the Delaware Valley Protective Association. The agency's diligence and commitment to keeping the canal from becoming a paved roadway resulted in the company gifting the canal to Pennsylvania. During the depths of the Depression, the Delaware Division Canal and the Lehigh Coal and Navigation Company deeded forty miles of canal and right-of-way to the people of Pennsylvania for use as a public park. The state renamed the waterway the Roosevelt State Park in 1940. This officially marked the end of an important era in American history.

In 1982, a group of committed volunteers formed the Friends of the Delaware Canal to continue to protect the canal and preserve its beauty. The canal was designated a National Historic Landmark in 1978, and in 1989 the name was changed from Roosevelt State Park to the Delaware Canal State Park.

At that time, Congress created the Delaware and Lehigh Navigation Canal National Heritage Corridor, which allows the National Park Service to assist state, local governments and agencies in the care and restoration of the canal.

As for the inns and taverns that provided for the bargemen, their families and the tourists who came to them on their "floating vacations," some have closed and others have changed their names and still serve tourists as bed-and-breakfasts and restaurants.

Every day, hikers, joggers and bicyclists use the towpath somewhere along its sixty-mile stretch. It's hard to imagine the days when the quiet water was congested with barges and the towpath crowded with mules and their drivers. There are stretches on the canal where the peaceful water mirrors the beauty of surrounding trees and foliage. It is a natural aviary for birds and fowl, and their songs can be almost symphonic along the calm canal. Unfortunately, there are long stretches where the water is drained and the canal has been damaged by recent floods; yet despite this, the towpath offers lovely views of the river in many areas, and it's no wonder that tourists flock to the inns and restaurants along the canal for the views it offers and the quiet peace it emanates.

The canal is a living entity, not just an obsolete method of transportation. Its quiet waters and lush vegetation sustain nature; its resilience provides a life force for those who draw from its peaceful beauty.

Epilogue

When I moved to Bucks County twenty years ago with my family, I was enthralled with this charming, beautiful place. It was thrilling to see that this county had carefully preserved many of the buildings that had housed people and events from as far back as the 1600s and that its history had been carefully documented and secured by the local historical societies.

The tiny stone buildings stand as erect and proud as the expansive mansions built in the succeeding periods of time. Townships and boroughs throughout Bucks County are vigilant about safeguarding their past through the preservation of their buildings, even as the region grows steadily with estate-sized homes built on what were just recently lush pastures.

Over the last twenty years, I've eaten at almost all the historic inns and taverns of Bucks County. Most of them are trendy upscale restaurants now that serve ten different versions of martinis instead of ale and hard cider; their chefs are internationally renowned, but just as in the 1600s, 1700s and 1800s, they are the "hot spots" of the region—the places to go, to be seen, to gossip and to enjoy a good meal.

History is visually present and beautifully maintained in Bucks County, just waiting for questions to be asked and stories to be told. I only wish I could have told all the stories and covered every Bucks County inn and tavern, but it would be impossible to do Bucks County justice in one book.

I want to thank again all of the people who have helped me with researching this book. I am in awe of their work in preserving and keeping local history safe so that all the generations to come will understand that even the smallest hamlets and quietest villages contributed to the growth of this wonderful country and played a role—indeed, continue to play a role—in America's history.

Notes

Introduction

1. Pennsylvania Historical and Museum Commission, "William Penn," http://www.phmc.state.pa.us/ppet/penn/page1.asp.
2. Quakers and the Political Process, "Penn's Holy Experiment: The Seed of a Nation," Philadelphia Yearly Meeting, http://www.pym.org/exhibit/p078.html.
3. Pennsylvania Historical and Museum Commission, "Pennsbury Manor: The Philosopher's Garden," http://www.phmc.state.pa.us/ppet/pennsbury/page1.asp.
4. W.W. Davis, *History of Bucks County* (New York and Chicago: Lewis Publishing, 1905), 149.
5. Ibid.
6. Albert Sidney Bolles, *Pennsylvania, Province and State: a history from 1609 to 1790* (Philadelphia, PA: Wanamaker, 1899), 118.

Chapter 1

7. J.H. Battle, *History of Bucks County, Pennsylvania* (Chicago: Warner & Co., 1887), 111.
8. Pennsylvania Historical and Museum Commission, "Pennsylvania's Roads Before the Automobile," http://www.phmc.state.pa.us/ppet/roads1/page1.asp.

Chapter 2

9. Willis M. Rivinus, *Early Taverns of Bucks County, 1965* (New Hope: n.p., 1965), 12.
10. Pennsbury Manor, Tour Information.
11. Rivinus, *Early Taverns*, 6.

Chapter 3

12. Digital History Online Textbook, "Toward Revolution," http://www.digitalhistory.uh.edu/historyonline/us6.cfm.

13. Bucks County Schools Intermediate Unit No. 22, "Bucks County Split by Tory and Rebel Sentiments," *Bucks County Chronicle* (1977): 84.
14. Thomas Paine, *The Crisis December 23, 1776*, Independence Hall Association, USHistory.com, http://www.ushistory.org/Paine/crisis/c-01.htm.
15. David McCullough, *1776* (New York: Simon & Schuster, 2005), 273.
16. William S. Striker, *The Battles of Trenton and Princeton* (Trenton, NJ: Old Barracks Association, 2001), 371.
17. Pennsylvania Historical and Museum Commission, "Letter from Washington to Continental Congress," http://www.ushistory.org/washingtoncrossing/history/account1.htm.
18. "The Times That Try Men's Souls: 1776–1777," *Liberty! The American Revolution*, DVD, directed by Ellen Hovde and Muffie Meyer (1997; Arlington, VA: PBS).
19. Pennsylvania Historical and Museum Commission, "Timeline: From Founding Through the American Revolution," http://ushistory.org/washingtoncrossing/history/revwartimeline.htm.
20. *Wikipedia, The Free Encyclopedia*, s.v. "Hessian," http://en.wikipedia.org/wiki/Hessian (accessed July 7, 2007).

Chapter 4

21. Benjamin West (American, worked in Britain, 1738–1820), *Elizabeth Shewell West and Her Son, Raphael*, ca.1770. Oil on canvas; 66.5 x 66.3 cm. ©The Cleveland Museum of Art, The Charles W. Harness Gift, 1927.

Chapter 5

22. Davis, *History of Bucks County*, 341.
23. Battle, *History of Bucks County*, 377.
24. Edward R. Barnsley, "Tavern Keepers Newtown 1739–1864" (Newtown Historic Association Research Center, n.d.).
25. Ibid.
26. Ibid.
27. According to Phrases.org.UK, John Heywood, the sixteenth-century collector of proverbs, recorded a version in his *A dialogue conteinyng the nomber in effect of all the prouerbes in the Englishe tongue, 1546*: "Better one byrde in hande than ten in the wood." The Bird in Hand was adopted as a pub name in the UK in the Middle Ages and there are still many pubs of that name there. This refers back to medieval falconry where a bird in the hand (the falcon) was certainly worth more than two in the bush (the prey). Phrases.org.UK, "A Bird in the Hand," ©Gary Martin, http://www.phrases.org.uk/meanings/64950.html.
28. Josiah B. Smith, *Historical Collections of Persons, Land, Business, and Events in Newtown* (Doylestown, PA: 1941), 159.
29. Edward R. Barnsley, *Historic Newtown* (Newtown, PA: n.p., 1934), 54.
30. Harry W. Van Horn, "The Battle Royal of the Civil War at the Township House" (Newtown Historic Association Research Center, Township House Vertical Files).
31. Ibid.

32. *Bucks County Courier Times*, "Focus on Newtown," August 27, 1998.
33. Barnsley, "Tavern Keepers."
34. Langhorne Centennial 1876–1976, "The Underground Railroad" (Newtown, PA: Advance of Bucks County, 1975), 45.
35. Robert Mettrick, "A History of Negro Voting in Pennsylvania During the Nineteenth Century" (PhD diss., Rutgers University, 1985), 22–25.

Chapter 6

36. Steve Wartenberg and Gian Luiso, *The Delaware Canal: Its Life, Its Legacy* (New Hope, PA: Friends of the Delaware Canal, 2000), 24.

Bibliography and Resources

"A Collection of Papers Read Before the Bucks County Historical Society." Vol. II. Riegelsville, PA: B.F. Fackenthal Jr., 1909.

———. Vol. V. Riegelsville, PA: Fackenthal Publication Fund, 1926.

American Revolution. "Insane King George III." Americans.net. http://www.americanrevolution.com/KingGeorge3rd.htm.

Barnsley, Edward R. *Historic Newtown.* Newtown, PA: n.p., 1934.

Bartholomew, Ann, and Lance E. Metz. *Delaware and Lehigh Canals*. Second Ed. Easton, PA: Canal History and Technology Press, 2005.

Battle, J.H., ed. *History of Bucks County Pennsylvania*. Chicago, IL: A. Warner & Co., 1887.

Bolles, Albert Sidney. *Pennsylvania, Province and State: a history from 1609 to 1790.* Philadelphia, PA: Wanamaker, 1899.

Bucks County Schools Intermediate Unit No. 22. *Bucks County Chronicles* (1977).

Cawley, James, and Margaret Cawley. *Along the Old York Road.* New Brunswick, NJ: Rutgers University Press, 1965.

Colonial National Historic Park. "Brewing In the Seventeenth Century: How It's Done." http://www.nps.gov/archive/colo/Jthanout/BREWING.html.

Davis, W.W.H., and A.M. *History of Doylestown, Old and New from its Settlement to the Close of the 19th Century, 1745–1900.* Doylestown, PA: Democrat Book and Job Office Print, 1876.

———. *The History of Bucks County Pennsylvania From the Discovery of the Delaware to the Present Time.* Doylestown, PA: Democrat Book and Job Office Print, 1876.

ExplorePAHistory.com. "Stories from PA History." WITF, Inc. http://www.explorepahistory.com/stories.php.

EyeWitness to History. "Washington Crosses the Delaware, 1776." Ibis Communications, Inc. http://www.eyewitnesstohistory.com/washingtondelaware.htm.

Ford, Alice. *Painter of the Peaceable Kingdom.* Philadelphia: University of Pennsylvania Press, 1952.

History of Early American Taverns. "Old Time Taverns." 20-20 Site. http://www.2020site.org/americantavern/oldtime.html.

History of Transport and Travel. "Carriages: 17 Century A.D." History World. http://www.historyworld.net/wrldhis/PlainTextHistories.asp?groupid=1972&HistoryID=ab79.

Lathrop, Elise. *Early American Inns and Taverns.* New York, NY: R.M. McBride & Co., 1926.

Lebegern, George F., Jr. *Episodes in Bucks County History: A Bicentennial Tribute 1776–1976.* Fallsington, PA: Bucks County Historical-Tourist Commission, 1975.

Marshall, Jeffrey L. *Early History of Upper Makefield Township Bucks County, PA.* Washington Crossing, PA: The Society, 1990.

Marshall, Jeffrey L., and Bertha S. Davis. *Wrightstown Township A Tricentennial History.* Wycombe, PA: Wrightstown Township Historical Commission, 1992.

Mayer, Thomas C. *A History of Land Ownership Newtown, Bucks County, Pennsylvania 1683–1850.* Bedminster, PA: Adams Apple Press, 1999.

McCullough, David. *1776.* New York, NY: Simon & Schuster, 2005.

McNealy, Terry A. *A History of Bucks County Pennsylvania.* Fallsington, PA: Bucks County Historical-Tourist Commission, 1970.

Muir, Dorothy Troth. *General Washington's Headquarters.* Troy, AL: Troy State University Press, 1977.

Myers, Albert Cooks. *Narratives of Early Pennsylvania West New Jersey and Delaware 1630–1707.* New York, NY: C. Scribner's, 1912.

Quakers and the Political Process: Living Our Faith into Action. "Penn's Holy Experiment: The Seed of a Nation 2000–2001." Philadelphia Yearly Meeting. http://www.pym.org/exhibit/p078.html.

Rice, Kym S. *Early American Taverns: for the entertainment of friends and strangers*. Chicago, IL: Regnery Gateway, 1983.

Rivinus, Marion Willis and Katharine Hansell Biddle. *Lights Along the Delaware.* Pittsburg, PA: Dorrance & Co., Inc., 1965.

Rivinus, Willis M. *Early Taverns of Bucks County*. New Hope, PA: n.p., 1965.

Smith, Eric Ledell. "The End of Black Voting Rights in Pennsylvania African Americans and the Pennsylvania Constitution of 1837–1838. *Pennsylvania History* 65 (Summer 1998): 279–299.

Thompson, Peter. *Rum Punch and Revolution: Taverngoing and Public Life in Eighteenth Century Philadelphia*. Philadelphia: University of Pennsylvania Press, 1999.

Thomspson, Ray. *The Walking Purchase Hoax of 1737*. Fort Washington, PA: Bicentennial Press, 1973.

Tise, Larry E. *Pennsbury Manor Pennsylvania Trail of History Guide.* Mechanicsburg, PA: Stackpole Books, 2002.

Tunis, Edwin. *The Tavern at the Ferry.* New York, NY: Crowell, 1973.

Index

J

K

L

M

N

P

R

S

T

U

W

Y